THE WISDOM OF A NIGHTINGALE

THE WISDOM OF A NIGHTINGALE

INSIGHTS AND TEACHINGS FROM A LIFE
OF VULNERABILITY, HOPE AND LOVE

MARY ANNE WILLOW
& JAMES WILLOW

Copyright © Mary Anne Willow 2025

24 23 22 21 20 19 18 17 16

Mary Anne Willow has asserted her right under the Copyright, Designs and Patent Act 1998 to be identified as the author of this work.
This book is sold subject to the condition that it shall not by way of trade or otherwise, be lent, resold, hired out, or otherwise circulated without the publisher's prior consent in any form of binding or cover other than that in which it is published and without similar condition including this condition being imposed on the subsequent purchaser.

This book recounts personal and intimate experiences and should be viewed as a subjective account of a personal journey of discovery. Although Mary Anne has taken care to verify that any factual information is accurate, for authoritative guides on the matters discussed, the reader should look elsewhere.

Some names and identifying features and some occupations have been modified or excluded to preserve anonymity. The purpose of this is to protect the privacy of the individual without damaging the integrity of the storytelling.

Art direction, cover design and all typography by Monomo & Co

Printed and bound in the UK. All paper sourced from wood grown in sustainable forests.

A CIP catalogue record for this book is available from the British Library

ISBN 978-1-7392561-2-8

www.maryannewillow.uk

Editor
Helen Fazal

I dedicate this book to my beloved grandparents Hilda and James. Through their love and devotion I discovered beauty, hope, love and grace.

They left this world a kinder place.

Contents

Preface	XIII
Introduction	XVII

Part I - The Power and Wisdom of Storytelling

The Unmothered Child	1
The Vulnerable Child	4
Cigarettes, Whisky and Firearms	9
Wild, Wayward and Wandering	14
Welsh Seagulls	18
Longing and Belonging	25
An Irreversible Ending	29
The Call of the Nightingale	33
Carpe Diem	38
Pride and Prestige	44
The Prelude to Illumination	50
Priests, Ships and Hounds	56
Paradox and Paranoia	62
Forgiving Dreams	69
Tormented to Death	75
Bare Dreams	80
The Prophecy is Realised	86
A Secret Lie	90
The Widowed Spinster	94
Sophia	101
An Invisible Loss	107
Herons and Horses	113
A Sanctimonious Halo	119
Surviving the Stitch-up and Smiling Through Pain	124
The Song of the Nightingale ~ After winter must come spring	133
Meditations	139

Part II - Echoes of Wisdom

A Deeper Understanding	145
Enlightenment, Compassion and Contentment	150
The Mystery, Magic and Wonder of Beauty	155
Amazing Grace – Awakening the Soul	157
The Power and Beauty of the Natural World	162
The Devotion of Animals	164
Pursue a Life of Culture	165
Dying, Death and Dust	167
Living With Integrity	168
The Wisdom of a Nightingale, a poem	170

◆~◆

Acknowledgements	173
The Nightingale	175
The Music of the Nightingale	177
Cover Design	179
Background Information	181
List of Helpful Organisations	188
Bibliography	193
Background Information References	197
Index of Themes	200
Themes by Chapter	202
Reviews for *The Grace of a Nightingale*	206
Notes	208

Have patience with everything that is unresolved in your heart and try to love the questions themselves, like locked rooms, like books written in a foreign tongue. Do not now strive to uncover answers: they cannot be given you because you have not been able to live them. And what matters is to live everything. Live the questions for now. Perhaps then you will gradually, without noticing it, live your way into the answer, one distant day in the future.

Rainer Maria Rilke
Letters to a Young Poet

Preface

This book is for all those whose hearts are always beckoning to learn, live and love more deeply. *The Wisdom of a Nightingale* has been written to encourage you to set out on a journey of self-discovery, a transformative journey that will enable you to see the shimmering divine presence in all things.

> *I write to you, not because you do not know the truth, but because you know it.*
> 1 John 2:21

The call to write this book began following the publication of my debut book *The Grace of a Nightingale: A Memoir of Vulnerability, Hope and Love* when I was often asked by readers: how did I cope?

So how did I cope with the different shapes and sizes of adversity which began with my earliest childhood memory at the age of three and persisted throughout my adult life? What has given me the ability to endure hardship, disappointment, suffering and loss without becoming distracted by self-pity, bitterness and resentment?

The answer is simple, yet profound and mysterious:

Love

I was comforted by the tenderness and alluring fragrance of a divine love which manifests herself in beauty, kindness, gentleness and forgiveness.

> *Beloved, let us love one another, because love is from God; everyone who loves is born of God and knows God. Whoever does not love does not know God, for God is love.*
> 1 John 4:7-9

When faced with seemingly unbearable circumstances, this love enabled me to believe my life could move from adversity to opportunity, from deprivation to prosperity, and that I could recover and heal from past hurts.

At the heart of my experience of this divine love was my connection with the natural world. Both human and animal love evoked a strong and powerful sense of determination to function and recover from tragedy, failure and suffering.

> *There was always a stronger light beckoning beyond the dark tunnel of fear and failure.*

In *The Wisdom of a Nightingale* I explore how past trauma, both physical and mental, is often concealed deep within and cannot be observed externally. Thus, to others I may seem healthy and 'walk cheerfully across the earth and touch that of God in everyone' but beneath the surface I struggle with an inner landscape scarred by abuse, tragedy and failure. I carry the wounds of harm and neglect.

In writing *The Grace of a Nightingale* I wanted to show readers how an inner sense of blessed trust enabled me to take risks in pursuit of my authentic self; how I chose to embrace a mysterious, deep-seeking inner wisdom in search of the true nature of love: love free of expectation and exploitation. My ability to endure misfortune was founded on a capacity for deep introspection, an evolving resilience, emotional self-sufficiency and compassionate empathy. Being denied affection as a child fostered each of these characteristics.

By telling my story I have reached a place of healing and peace, enabling me to be restored to my true self, the person I was intended to become. I have discovered my own distinct identity and discarded false beliefs shaped by misjudgement, abuse and oppression. My journey has enabled me to be inspired to see God in all things. Despite great suffering I have been blessed with a deeper self-discovery, radical hope and divine love.

> *There is a constant mystical thread, a deep longing which is found within human vulnerability. It is a soulful desire for union with the divine which manifests herself in nature and human life.*

The Wisdom of a Nightingale is a more considered response to the question: how did I cope? It attempts to describe the compelling insights and lessons I have come to know through misfortune, faith and love.

Throughout Parts I and II, I offer you carefully considered incisive questions, mindful reflection exercises and meditations. These are to help deepen your self-awareness, consider your relationships and enable you to examine your life experience. They are intended to inspire and empower you to live more freely and more happily.

> *Man was made for joy and woe;*
> *and when this we rightly know,*
> *thro' the world we safely go.*
> *Joy and woe are woven fine,*
> *a clothing for the soul divine*
>
> **William Blake**
> Auguries of Innocence

Mary Anne Willow, January 2025

Introduction

What are your deepest longings, hopes and fears? Do you yearn to live more freely, healed and detached from negative emotions: resentment, grief, fear, jealousy, anger, low self-esteem? Do you want some control over the remnants of past hurts and disappointments? Are you searching for a remedy to convert sad memories into happy memories? Are you willing to consider questions which could be challenging and uncomfortable? It is my intention that this book will inspire you to respond 'yes' to these questions and take you on a life-transforming journey of discovery in search of your true authentic self.

It takes courage and trust to embark on a path which can be uncertain and daunting. It can be scary to step out into the unknown and feel the pain of letting go of what seems to be the foundation of your security, significance and self-worth. When reading my story you may come to recognise something about yourself which you haven't yet met.

Should you choose to read on, then this invitation will guide you to places of deeper understanding and empathy, self-awareness and wisdom.

Remember, all that I offer is based on my own personal journey.

Who is This Book For?

The Wisdom of a Nightingale is a companion to my memoir *The Grace of a Nightingale*. It is written from the heart for you as you set out on your own journey. This may be on your own, or it could involve a friend, mentor, minister, or small group. For example, it could be used as a weekly study guide for a church group that meets during Lent to deepen their faith and relationships with each other.

How to Use This Book

It is not essential to have read my memoir; this book can be read and applied independently. To help those who are not familiar with my story, in Part l James revisits each chapter and summarises key events. He has purposefully written in a way that offers the reader an objective description of each character and situation. He describes the context and detail without judgement and bias.

In Part I – The Power and Wisdom of Storytelling each chapter summary is followed by a section headed 'Intuitive Wisdom'. This is the distillation of my lifelong learning: what I have come to know from specific periods of my life, regardless of my age, circumstances and challenges. Sometimes these points were apparent at the time; others occurred to me later in life, through therapy, meditation, reading, prayer, study, the influence of my mat carriers, both human and animal, or even triggered by further trauma. There was a recurring realisation and recognition that I was not alone; neither was I too weak and worthless not to rise above adversity if I chose to. These insights sustained me and gave me the patience and perseverance to carry on, despite my vulnerability and lost hopes and dreams.

You may find these stories elicit a personal response through your own unique emotions and thoughts. As they resonate with your past experiences, you may encounter an unknown inner disturbance: past hurts and forgotten memories may be reawakened. I would encourage you to reflect on such experiences to discover a deeper wondrous inner knowing and freedom. You may also recognise hidden gifts and radical hope previously buried by fear, insecurity or self-limiting false beliefs.

If at any time you begin to feel overwhelmed then please stop. Don't continue alone but seek the support of someone you trust, perhaps a professional such as your GP, minister or counsellor. I have included a list of helpful organisations towards the end of this book. There is also a comprehensive index of themes should you wish to first judge the suitability of the subject matter before deciding whether to read on.

Lastly, for each chapter you will find a series of questions under the heading 'Developing Deeper Consciousness and Taking Compassionate Action'. These questions are designed to help you reflect on how *The Wisdom of a Nightingale* may have influenced you. There are no right or wrong answers. The questions are intended to evoke a response from which you can learn more about yourself, your relationships and life around you, beginning with the people and events who formed your early influences. The past cannot be changed, but you can change your perception.

After reading each chapter, I suggest you pause and take some private time to work through the questions. Before beginning the next chapter of your choice you may wish to concentrate on the Mindful Reflection at the end of this Introduction or the Meditations, which can be found at the end of the first part of the book. This can be alone or with a companion or discussion group.

Although Part 1 is structured chronologically according to my memoir, it is not imperative that you follow this pathway. You can dip in and out of different sections and chapters according to your preference. This book is not intended to be prescriptive but to encourage flexible reading and reflection on your needs and longings, awakening your own seeing, hearing and knowing. I hope you find this thought-provoking and stimulating. May I encourage you to let your inner voice be your guide, according to your hopes and dreams.

> *Listen deeply as your soul gently whispers which way to travel in search of glimpses of wisdom embraced in the story of your life.*

Take time to reflect on your life and discover fresh insights about your journey. This process is intended to enable you to identify significant events in your life so you can create a more integrated sense of who you are. Patterns may emerge that help you understand yourself more deeply.

The discovery of the invisible truths about who you are can be challenging, revealing distorted thinking patterns and unhelpful assumptions. You may now want to alter these to improve your feelings and your decision-making: to replace self-limiting assumptions and beliefs with ones which inspire and empower you.

> *Knowledge of the self is the mother of all knowledge. So it is incumbent on me to know my self, to know it completely, to know its minutiae, its characteristics, its subtleties, and its very atoms.*
>
> **Kahlil Gibran**
> The Prophet

The second part of the book is called 'Echoes of Wisdom'. As I wrote Part 1, revisiting my story chapter by chapter, I found that certain themes recurred, timeless echoes accompanying me throughout my life, such as beauty, grace, and nature. The intent of these echoes was constant: a call to abandon fear, arrogance and conceit and fall in love with the wonder of the divine.

These themes are like the continuous threads of a beautiful tapestry which twist and weave their way across the landscape of my journey. By gazing at their pattern and texture I discovered deeper self-knowledge and understanding. They became an intuitive wisdom which guided, strengthened and consoled me during times of worry, struggle and confusion. They helped me make some sense of my experiences and find deeper meaning from the rhythm of my life. Moreover, I discovered a deeper intimacy with nature, beauty and the divine.

Come with me and let me share my lived experiences. Written from the heart, *The Wisdom of a Nightingale* will gently guide you along a journey of discovery, enlightenment, learning and choice.

> *He has told you, O mortal, what is good;*
> *and what does the Lord require of you*
> *but to do justice, and to love kindness,*
> *and to walk humbly with your God?*
> **Micah 6:8**

Mindful Reflection

As you read the story of my life in Part 1, I encourage you to pause for reflection at the end of each chapter.

Sit down alone and in silence.

Close your eyes and lower your head.

Breathe out gently and imagine yourself looking into your own heart.

Reflect on what you have read and consider what fresh insights you have gained about yourself, your relationships and your life.

What emerging patterns and themes, if any, do you notice?

What did you find challenging?

What did you find inspiring?

How will these influence any future similar situations and choices?

What would you like to STOP doing, KEEP doing and START doing?

Note: Mindful reflection is like having a conversation with yourself. It encourages you to analyse your thoughts, emotions and body in a non-judgemental way. Through this you can develop greater self-awareness and a deeper understanding of your true, authentic self. Meditation involves focusing on one thing and tuning out any distractions. This can enable you to develop deeper calmness and concentration. Both mindful reflection and meditation can help with your wellbeing.

A pattern is a recurring way of behaving in a situation or towards people. For example, you find you are much more comfortable in smaller groups whereas in large groups you tend to be quiet and withdrawn. Or perhaps you are happier when you are by the sea opposed to being in a busy town or city.

Themes are your motivational goals, such as love, finding fulfilling work, being kind to others, truth and justice.

Mat Carriers

I use the term 'mat carrier' to describe those individuals, both human and animal, who have supported me through life and given me strength to carry on. Based on the New Testament story of the paralysed man whose friends lowered him through the roof to hear Jesus speak, this term tells of how others can carry us to Jesus when we are too sick and weak to help ourselves. I am moved by the perseverance, ingenuity and faith of the man's friends.

Through Jesus we find healing and hope when life seems desolate. When I reflect on how I survived a childhood of severe neglect and abuse and further suffering and disappointments, this story explains how the love of others has undoubtedly carried me, helping me to find the courage and hope to keep going and the belief that life can get better.

> *And I saw the river*
> *over which every soul must pass*
> *to reach the kingdom of heaven*
> *and the name of that river was suffering:*
> *and I saw a boat that carries souls across the river*
> *and the name of that boat was*
> *love.*
>
> **St John of the Cross**
> Spiritual Canticle

As you read the book you may wish to reflect on this term. Have there been times when you have become a mat carrier for others? Or perhaps you have been carried to places of beauty, hope, healing and peace by the love and faith of your own mat carriers.

A Note on Quotations

In the following pages I have shared many quotations from *The Grace of a Nightingale* to connect you more intimately with certain aspects of my story. These stand alone without attribution. What I discovered when writing these was an endless creative instinct to refine the words and sentences. My desire to convey in some new way extracts from *The Grace of a Nightingale* sometimes means these quotations are altered. I could not resist the urge to craft my writing in order to add freshness and originality.

All quotations from the Bible are taken from the New King James Version.

Part I

The Power and Wisdom of
Story Telling

Chapter 1

The Unmothered Child
(1962 – 1969)

Mary Anne was born into a volatile and fragile household. She had to endure her parents' dysfunctional relationship, which was often abusive, both mentally and physically. Some of this abuse was aimed at Mary Anne and was a constant threat. Her earliest memory, aged three, is not of balloons or birthday cake; it is visceral and violent. Seared into her mind is the image of her father, like a deranged animal, beating her mother with one of her own wooden heeled pink slippers.

Her mother began to use Mary Anne as her emotional punch bag. In contrast, she idolised Mary Anne's brother, Lee, who was eighteen months younger. This was a pattern that would continue throughout her life.

Mary Anne's first home was in a small rural Yorkshire village where she relished peace and tranquillity, blotting out her troubled home life with precious moments of solitude, outside in the fields behind her house listening to birdsong, or in bed at night cocooned under her favourite pink blanket. She was both blessed and cursed with being sensitive and self-aware from an early age. This was the burgeoning of her individuality and strong moral compass. She instinctively knew right from wrong.

Even at this young age, Mary Anne understood that she must not and would not resemble her parents.

Intuitive Wisdom

By looking back into our early childhood memories, we can begin to understand ourselves more deeply, growing in consciousness and self-awareness. Exploring our earliest recollections provides a window into our life patterns. This is a process of discovery whereby false beliefs shaped by abuse and oppression can be shed.

───

It is a natural human need to want to grow in knowledge, consciousness and identity.

───

We are not owned by our parents. We are part of a bigger life force.

We are not beholden to our parents.

We can be grateful to our parents.

We can love and care for them without guilt, which can be harmful over a long period of time.

───

Children are to be respected, loved, cherished and protected.

When a child's only protector is physically or emotionally threatening, this can affect their development.

Even very young children can discern adults' temperaments: whether they are good and kind or nasty and cruel.

Do not assume those who we believe love us by virtue of familiarity will not harm or hurt us. It can be quite the opposite.

A frightened child can find an imaginative safe place in nature. Time spent in wild spaces can bring freedom from anxiety, solace and peace.

Developing Deeper Consciousness and Taking Compassionate Action

What are your earliest memories?

Which of these have shaped or influenced your life?

How do these memories create defensive and protective thoughts?

Self-awareness is a gift which can seem magical to others. Learn to develop it, so you will notice both the surface but also what is going on deep down.

⁓

Despite the difficult circumstances at home, I discovered the beauty of nature and outdoors.

> *I remember playing in yellow cornfields at the end of our back garden. I would make dens there, peaceful, quiet retreats where the secret invisible beauty of birdsong brought an atmosphere of hope and calm. As I nestled in the safe shelter of high, sweet-smelling golden stalks, I daydreamed about living in a faraway place surrounded by green hills, forests, silver flowing streams and colourful wildlife.*

Take some quiet time to recall the sense of beauty and wonder you felt as a child.

How does this sense of childhood wonder influence your life today?

What does nature mean to your adult self?

Chapter 2

The Vulnerable Child
(1969 – 1973)

⁓

The family move from Yorkshire to the northwest of England, leaving behind a quiet rural setting to live on a new housing development in an ugly industrial town.

In her new home Mary Anne felt unsafe. She had swapped green fields for a building site to play in. At school the children were unruly and she struggled to understand the dialect. She was bullied by one of the girls in her class.

As she grew, she and her friends encountered predatory sexual behaviour in a variety of situations: the local swimming pool, walking home from school, even from a neighbour. They were reluctant to tell adults for fear of being blamed.

Family income became tight when Mary Anne's father was caught up in a bitter industrial dispute that caused severe financial problems for the household. This put even more strain on the family dynamics.

The one advantage of moving to this area was that Mary Anne's maternal grandparents lived close by. They doted on their granddaughter, cradling her in their love, and providing an island of calm in an otherwise turbulent existence. They showed her how to live with grace and kindness. Lacking material wealth, their richness was their love and devotion. Witnessing this was hugely significant for Mary Anne.

Walks with her grandfather in the local park opened Mary Anne's mind to the healing power of nature. She loved running errands for her grandparents' elderly neighbour to the corner shop. She discovered the joy to be gained from helping others.

> *Helping others made me feel alive. I was energised, and I began to feel a sense of connection to others.*

Mary Anne's grandparents were the parents she should have had, a beacon of light and hope. Without this deep attachment it is unlikely she would have been able to survive as well as she did; she may have been troubled by the wounds of abuse in ways that blocked her ability to find her heart's desire for happiness, fulfilment, safety, and security: to love and be loved.

This is the point at which the developing characters of Mary Anne and her brother Lee begin to significantly diverge. Lee revelled in causing trouble, chaos and mischief, which seemed to be encouraged by their parents. Mary Anne knew she wanted to be different: gentle, thoughtful, kind, truthful and loving, like her grandparents.

She discovered the joy to be found from reading, identifying with fictional characters such as Paddington and Anne, in *Anne of Green Gables*. Listening to music, too, provided a temporary escape from reality.

Intuitive Wisdom

> *Grandad and I went for walks in the local park with its natural woodland area. There was an abundance of springtime flowers, an endless carpet of bluebells, their beauty bursting into life with a fresh, youthful scent.*

This first knowing encounter with such beauty was a gentle awakening to a divine passion.

―✧―

We are morally obliged to love our children unconditionally. They should be protected and cared for, and always deserve our respect and acceptance.

―✧―

When children move house they may grieve for the loss of routine and familiarity: friends, school and play areas. There is a moving scene depicting this in Kenneth Branagh's film Belfast. Due to escalating violence in 1960s Northern Ireland, nine-year-old

Buddy's Ma and Pa decided to leave Belfast for a new life in England. Buddy was distraught and strongly against this, especially as it meant separation from his beloved grandparents.

～

Children need to play and explore the outdoors, even when the environment is unfit and unsafe. This is clearly demonstrated in Paul Trevor's documentary photographs of Liverpool street kids in the 1970s.

～

Children are vulnerable to sexual predators, even in open and public places, and not only by strangers but also by friends/family/neighbours.

Children are likely to believe it is their fault when abused and violated. This silences them and prevents them telling an adult. If their parent/primary carer is aggressive this may also prevent a child from confiding in them, for fear of further violence towards them and their abuser.

～

Parental favouritism can create harmful sibling rivalry, abuse and ultimately estrangement.

Children from the same family can experience very different childhoods. They are not equal. Birth order means that each will have different roles and responsibilities.

～

The power of emotional attachment to grandparents by grandchildren is not to be underestimated. This can provide some compensation for inadequate parenting.

Grandparents can influence and inspire grandchildren in ways that enable them to be open to creativity, nature, beauty, joy and love.

～

Natural beauty awakens the divine passion within. The frightened child can create a safe place in their mind, a soothing place of rivers and streams, mountains, trees and wildlife.

Helping others can make us happy, grateful and feel more alive.

Engaging with fictional characters can help children to be happy.

Developing Deeper Consciousness and Taking Compassionate Action

> *The joy of giving was far stronger than the worry of poverty. There was always enough when we needed it.*

Identify your earliest memory of being kind to someone.

How did this make you feel?

How has being kind to others influenced your life?

How can we as a society encourage one another to show greater kindness?

What qualities do you admire and respect in family members and friends?

Which fictional characters influenced your childhood?

Describe your imaginary experiences when playing in nature as a child.

> *I would run errands for her to Brown's, the corner shop, to be rewarded with a threepenny bit, a kind word and a grateful smile.*

Consider the joy of thanksgiving. Practise expressing gratitude now!

Identify those people, circumstances and opportunities for which you are genuinely grateful and give thanks.

Chapter 3

Cigarettes, Whisky and Firearms

(1973 – 1976)

Already chaotic, Mary Anne's home life now descended into hell. She suffered the loss of an angel and was groomed by a demon. Nanna was found to have cancer and died after an agonising period of illness. Jealous of Mary Anne's close relationship with her grandmother, Mum forced her daughter to touch Nanna's body as it lay in an open coffin, knowing how distressed she would be.

Nanna's painful death was hugely significant and still resonates today. She was the cradle of love and devotion in Mary Anne's young life. As well as the trauma of losing this sweet woman, her beloved mother figure, Mary Anne had also lost her emotional support. After the death of his wife, her grandad was broken, lonely and isolated.

Within this period of grief Mary Anne was groomed by Trevor, a cunning and manipulative paedophile she encountered when babysitting. After attempting to tell her GP of the abuse, who accused her of making up stories to seek attention, Mary Anne told no one, fearing she would be branded a liar or a fantasist. She felt trapped. She began to lose respect for authority figures, such as doctors and teachers. No one showed concern; no one rescued her from her tormentors.

She started secondary school, which she remembers as a place of harm and abuse, although friends from the time have more positive recollections. She witnessed cruel corporal punishment from a sadistic teacher called Mr Naylor.

She experienced a premonition that her brother would come to harm. Later that day Lee was knocked over by a car and taken to hospital with a broken leg.

Her mother's mental health worsened as she became addicted to cigarettes, alcohol and prescription drugs. She also started to flirt and develop sexual relationships with other men, including Trevor. Her volatility and violence towards Mary Anne increased.

However, there were two things that Mary Anne was thankful for: she started to menstruate heavily, which halted the advances of the paedophile, and she was sent to an all-girls school which focused on high academic achievement. Her new school offered a calmer environment without physical punishment.

Intuitive Wisdom

> *The mind is its own place, and in itself can make a Heaven of Hell, a Hell of Heaven.*
> **John Milton**
> Paradise Lost

Two people can have completely different perceptions of the same experience, as with Mary Anne's experience of her first senior school.

※

> *What was Mr Naylor saying to himself? Was he projecting his own self-loathing and hatred onto the child, declaring: If I can hurt inside then so can you.*

Unresolved childhood pain and suffering can later be transmitted onto others, including children, to avenge deep-rooted past humiliations. This can be true of teachers, parents and those in authority.

Children who experience humiliation at school from insensitive teachers will learn it is not safe to make a mistake.

※

Can sibling intuition serve as a warning against danger? Shared formative experiences can create strong sibling–sibling emotional bonds. Deep sibling bonding can provide support and help the child to survive. This is an emotionally complex interpersonal relationship.

> *One sunny day I glanced out of my bedroom window to see Lee playing on his skateboard. I had a strange, uncomfortable feeling. Something horrid was going to happen to him. My sense of knowing had come to warn me.*

Domestic abuse is a breeding ground for further trauma and grooming. A child growing up in an abusive home is vulnerable: lack of protection and their need for attachment can place them at risk. They are more likely to find themselves in dangerous situations.

Loss of a beloved spouse can leave the surviving partner grief-stricken, socially isolated, lonely and depressed.

> *Love knows not its own depth until the hour of separation.*
> **Kahlil Gibran**
> The Prophet

The reality of the anguish of acute grief cannot be known fully before the loss of our loved one. Nor do we fully know the depth of our love until that final parting. These can only be experienced after they have died, which can be shocking, heartbreaking and debilitating.

> *His life was now empty, stripped of the woman who had shown him the highest form of love and devotion. Her absence would leave him lonely and isolated. He was like a wandering, lost ghost, not quite dead and hauntingly sad.*

If childhood abuse goes unreported and remains hidden, children are often left believing the abuse was their fault. They can be silenced by fear, shame and blame. As adults they may go on to suffer from complex PTSD.

Shame isolates and silences. It can leave children feeling lonely and helpless.

Children from abusive homes will idealise their abusers – usually their parents – in order to survive and avoid shame. They normalise the abnormal.

While showing concern for all family members, those in authority (teachers, police officers, social workers, lawmakers) must ensure that the wellbeing and protection of the vulnerable child always comes first.

Failure to believe children who attempt to seek help can leave them with lifelong mistrust of those in authority.

Despite pain and suffering, children still have an innate ability to seek out exciting adventures through the imagination.

Developing Deeper Consciousness and Taking Compassionate Action

> *I ran out of the house crying and distraught, overcome with fear and grief. My world felt cold, empty and devoid of any tender loving care. The most kind-hearted person I knew was dead.*

If you found out that someone you loved very much was going to die tomorrow, what would you want to be sure you say to them today?

What would you want to hear them say to you?

> *After my first evening of babysitting, Trevor walked me home. He was drunk and giddy. As we approached the front door he started to kiss me. He began to say how excited he was that I could become his special babysitter, so special he was*

> *going to give me a lot of money. He pushed a five pound note and some change into my hand. It was a fortune to me. Frozen in the darkness of this unlawful moment I held out my hand, not knowing if this were a gift or a tainted curse.*

Describe your understanding of child grooming.

What circumstances place children at risk of being groomed?

If you suspected a child was at risk what action would you take?

What can we do as a society to prevent this and help others become more aware?

Chapter 4

Wild, Wayward and Wandering
(1976 – 1979)

Mary Anne's defiance of authority was deepening against all those people and institutions that were letting her down. She became both wayward and empowered, exploring her own individuality in search of excitement and freedom from abuse and oppression. At school her behaviour was deteriorating. Her chaotic home life made it difficult to concentrate or to complete homework. The teachers were sarcastic and showed no concern for her welfare.

Although still sensitive, nervous and frightened, Mary Anne decided she would have to determine her own future. She found part-time work in the local indoor market where she earned money and gained some independence.

At weekends she stayed with friends to avoid being at home. In each case the main attraction was their loving mother. Mary Anne refused to join her family on holiday. Instead, she created her own outdoor adventures. Nature was becoming ever more important to her and she loved to spend time at the local reservoir.

Even though she describes herself as wild and wayward, Mary Anne always knew right from wrong. She realised she needed to become serious about her education if she was to escape the life she was submerged in. She even investigated the option of being fostered so she could live in a calm, safe environment where she could study. This showed unusual maturity for a girl in her early teens. However, her father persuaded her to stay in the family home; he would be unable to cope with his domestic responsibilities without her help.

Meanwhile, Lee spent his time joyriding, drinking and stealing. Unlike his sister, he needed to be part of a gang.

Music was becoming increasingly important in Mary Anne's life.

Lyrics, chords and rhythms provided a form of revelatory and inspirational learning.

Intuitive Wisdom

> *So, troubled and lost, I carried on defying dogmatic state instruction, replacing it with a wandering search for hope and love. Deep within the alcoves of my heart, a compelling energy blinded me to the peril of my ways.*

To live where we do not belong is far worse than wandering about lost and lonely, longing to find safe attachment and our soulful kinship.

Teenagers will seek out comfort, care and compassion from substitute mothers.

Vulnerable children are at risk of joining perilous groups for validation and affirmation, even putting their lives in danger through reckless juvenile bravery.

※

Children can become disillusioned by their education when it is dry and uninspiring.

Teachers can fail to notice the declining welfare and academic performance of children, despite clear signs of disengagement: thrill-seeking, mischievousness and disruptive behaviour.

Classroom sarcasm is hurtful and wounding, intended to humiliate. Is this the way teachers try to avenge their own unresolved psychic pain? We always have a choice: either to transmit or transform our pain.

We can ask with a heart of compassion if a teacher's failure to notice childhood abuse may be due to inexperience, excessive workload, fear of conflict, or lack of management support. Is it a competence, capability or organisational culture problem?

Remember, whatever unkind version of you others create in their mind is not your responsibility.

> *It was during one of these tempestuous evenings, weary and desolate, gazing out into a moonless night, that I had a life-changing experience. It's strange how wisdom visits when things seem utterly hopeless.*

True wisdom can begin to emerge in a young person's life, allowing them to instigate change, such as finding employment, a safe place to live, recognising and dealing with abuse, pursuing an education and training.

Young adults from difficult backgrounds, with the right support, can make life-changing decisions.

> *I needed to get away. Away from the chaotic, harmful abuse and the abusers.*

Developing Deeper Consciousness and Taking Compassionate Action

> *During those long summer days of 1976, I decided to get a job. I wanted to work and earn money. A powerful survival instinct was telling me I needed to be capable of generating an income. If I could get myself a Saturday job, then it would get me out of the house, and I would have my own money, making me less dependent on my parents.*

In this chapter I start to discover my own individuality and self-determination. Despite my young age, I am aware that I have choices and can begin to make my own decisions.

When did you first become aware of your own individuality and self-determination?

What choices and decisions did you make? Describe the opportunities and achievements you experienced. Were there any frustrations?

These women carried me with their care and compassion, despite their own burdens and difficulties. I was mourning the loss of my Nanna. They were a substitute for the mum I longed for; they mothered me and became my secret mat carriers. They carried me with their love, and I let them feed and nurture me.

Who did you choose to spend time with as a teenager?

Why did you choose their company?

How has this influenced who you are today?

Looking back on your teenage years, would you make different choices regarding who you spent time with?

I slept beside the tranquil misty waters of the reservoir. I was being invited into the peaceful beauty of Nature as she held and comforted me in her soothing bosom. I was oblivious of any danger, and this allowed me to escape the tyranny of home and all its turbulence.

During the long hot summer of 1976 I planned secret adventures. I was becoming wild-hearted and reckless.

Describe some of the exciting adventures you had growing up.

What did you learn from these adventures?

How do these memories inspire and influence you today?

Chapter 5

Welsh Seagulls
(1979 – 1980)

Mary Anne was invited to spend the May bank holiday with a friend's family in their caravan in Wales. This gave her the idea of pursuing employment far away from home and she decided to seek a summer job in one of the sea-front hotels.

The experience of Wales was a revelation to Mary Anne: the hotel, the beautiful location, the wildlife, and being by the sea.

> *My soul was free to dance and celebrate. At last I was experiencing a sense of equanimity. This encounter with the life and rhythms of the coast stirred my soul and imagination. At last I could luxuriate in a place of timeless peace and calm. I had found a shelter where I could belong.*

Alan and Brenda, the hotel owners, offered genuine care and concern for the wellbeing of their employees. Mary Anne felt that she mattered. She valued her employers' boundaries, discipline and training. She took pride in her work and discovered she had a strong work ethic. Her self-esteem and self-worth grew. Alan and Brenda became mat carriers.

Her work taught Mary Anne many lessons, not least that the misfortunes of others could also have befallen her. Two such life lessons involved her co-workers at the hotel, Jane and Gareth. Jane was recovering from the physical and emotional effects of an abusive relationship and a recent abortion. In this vulnerable state she was befriended by a Turkish man who showered her with gifts, made her feel special, and offered to take her on a trip abroad to his hometown. Jane was overwhelmed and flattered. She ignored Alan and Brenda's concerns and travelled to Turkey. Before her flight home she was arrested at a

Turkish airport with drugs hidden in her suitcase, drugs she knew nothing about.

Gareth was an orphan with acute learning difficulties. Without Alan and Brenda's support – providing him with lodgings and paid work in the hotel – he may well have been living on the streets. Despite his challenging behaviour Alan and Brenda were committed to looking after him. Mary Anne was impressed by their selfless devotion.

> *In different ways, Jane and Gareth's stories taught me how easily other people's misfortunes could be mine; I was aware that 'there by the grace of God go I'. I too could make choices which could lead to all kinds of problems: unwanted pregnancy, drug and alcohol abuse, homelessness, destitution and social isolation. Random circumstances over which I would have no control could disadvantage me. None of us is immune to the misfortunes of life.*

Mary Anne's values and beliefs were constantly being challenged. A powerful memory is the story of Mr and Mrs Williams, a quiet couple who had been visiting the hotel for years. One morning Mr Williams was found dead in his bed and Mrs Williams had fled the hotel. The sudden death was of natural causes but it transpired that the couple were married, just not to each other.

> *We were shocked and saddened by this sudden death, as we were all fond of this quiet couple. It was also upsetting to see how their infidelity caused such misery for two families whose lives would be affected forever by what had happened. The memories of happy times would now be exchanged for the pain of broken trust and rejection. Could they have been happily married if they were capable of such calculated acts of disloyalty? Was neither of them concerned that their deceit might cause pain for their respective partners?*

In Wales Mary Anne felt happier and less anxious. She learned that she had the power to determine her attitude towards others and life in general. She was starting to discover her true self and took great care in getting to know herself in more depth, understanding her own worth and learning that she was motivated by beauty, kindness, compassion and a desire to serve others.

Intuitive Wisdom

> *The threshold to your soul is awakened as your senses become alive to wild coastal beauty which offers fragrant sea air, rolling waves, the call of sea birds and an endless blue horizon.*

A strong sense of self-determination is important for creating a fulfilling life.

Adverse childhood experiences can help create a 'tenacious survivor' who perseveres in the face of adversity.

※

Hard work can be empowering and transformational.

Healing and development takes place when we are valued and respected.

Supportive employers have the power to enable employees to reach their full potential.

The three S's of self-worth, security and service can come from choosing work which offers purpose and meaning.

Develop your sense of duty and love for one another.

Lived values, such as loyalty, dedication, kindness and commitment, can build stronger healthier relationships and lasting happiness.

※

Infidelity is painful and harmful for all concerned. It can have a ripple effect with unintended consequences.

※

Vulnerable young adults are at risk of grooming, which can have lifetime harmful repercussions.

Let us grow a society that wants to care for the less fortunate: the poor, vulnerable, powerless and sick.

Insight and understanding into the misfortunes of others helps to avoid the distractions of self-pity, envy and resentment and instead evokes a heart of kindness, compassion and benevolence.

✧

Try to avoid a fatalistic tone, moaning and self-pity. These fruitless characteristics only seek to collude with misery and undermine any conveyance of inspiration.

Take quiet time to reflect on your life. Develop a positive and empowered narrative with optimism and hope.

Past hurts and unresolved pain can be transformed into peaceful loving acceptance.

Reflect on everyday experiences and early recollections to discover a deeper wondrous inner knowing and freedom: 'know thyself.' There is treasure within. You will discover hidden gifts, radical hope and freedom from fear, insecurity and self-limiting false beliefs.

Trust in the mystery of your life.

Developing Deeper Consciousness and Taking Compassionate Action

> *I was offered employment from June to September 1979. This would be one of the defining periods of my life, rich with beauty, wisdom and love. I was able to convince Dad it was a good idea as it would only be for the summer period, but in truth I had a powerful urge to get right away.*

Describe your first experience of employment.

What did you most enjoy about it?

What did you least enjoy about it?

What did you learn about yourself from the experience?

How did it influence your subsequent choices of education and employment?

> *I was motivated to work hard. It wasn't because we were praised, promoted or rewarded financially, but because I discovered I had a natural desire to do my best. I had a work ethic.*

What motivates you at work?

What demotivates you at work?

How would you describe a good employer?

Are there any changes you would like to make to your current employment?

If this is something you would like to pursue, what action do you need to take to enable this to happen?

> *I didn't dwell on my dismal circumstances at home but felt blessed and fortunate. I had an increased ability to view my life with optimism and hope. I felt humbled and enlightened. My enthusiasm for the future was growing. Instead of feeling like a powerless victim, I was realising how privileged and fortunate I was. I had opportunities and choices which were no longer limited by my own thoughts.*

Identify a time in your life when you felt optimistic, hopeful and fortunate.

What can you do to minimise your dismal thoughts and encourage a sense of optimism, hope and good fortune?

> *An inner transformation was taking place, and I started to shed some of the resentments and bitterness I harboured towards others. I felt happier and less anxious. I was learning that I was free to determine my own attitude, regardless of my circumstances. There was no reason why I should be demoralised and unhappy.*

Describe a time in your life when you felt resentful and bitter towards others, perhaps trapped by people or circumstances.

What happened? Were you able to regain your sense of personal power?

What would you do differently in a similar situation?

Can you identify any negative thoughts, behaviours and emotions which are self-limiting?

How can you deal with these?

❧

Identify the significant turning points which have shaped your life.

Which of these did you make based on your best choices?

Were any of these choices made by others? Can you identify a life choice you made simply because you were expected to?

Can you identify any mat carriers who helped and affirmed you?

❧

> *What had I learned about myself so far? I'd discovered that I enjoyed helping people; I had found inner contentment and harmony from serving others. My self-confidence was growing. I had a purpose.*

Can you describe a time when you have been involved in serving others?

What effect did this have on your motivation and self-esteem?

Identify ways in which you can add meaning and value to your work and life by serving others.

> *This time of withdrawal and contemplation became a glistening revelation. I felt excited and alert, despite not knowing what future treasures were awaiting me. I had no fixed images to dream about.*

Becoming fully human often involves natural contemplation. Take a few minutes each day to develop a contemplative mind so that you can awaken to a more caring, loving and compassionate world.

> *At the end of the summer season I reluctantly returned home. I felt angry about leaving my seaside retreat, but somehow I knew that all would be well. I began to trust in the mystery of my life.*

Self-discipline and delayed gratification – the ability to resist an immediate reward in favour of a more valuable reward later — will prove to be in your best interests. The outcomes will prove to be more significant and rewarding.

Describe some examples of delayed gratification from your own life. How did you benefit from them?

Can you think of a time when you sought instant gratification and experienced regret because of it?

Chapter 6

Longing and Belonging
(1980)

As Mary Anne returned from the time of self-discovery, peace and tranquillity she had experienced in Wales to the ongoing abusive turmoil at home, she realised that she had to get away.

Reluctantly, she returned to school to study A Levels but struggled to tolerate the ridicule and sarcasm of the teachers in a culture of male dominance. At home she tried to cope with the mess and madness as her parents and brother continued with their chaotic, abusive and dysfunctional lives. Her mother was now an alcoholic who was frequently admitted to the local psychiatric hospital, while Lee had been expelled from school. The self-esteem Mary Anne had gained from working and living in Wales began to ebb away. Despite her turbulent home life Mary Anne's determination to create a better future was unwavering. She chose to trust deeply and be optimistic despite the mess around her and not knowing what the future held.

> *I started to be comfortable with the uncertainty of not knowing what the future was preparing for me. I had a sense of expectation. My silent destiny was being created. Alchemic magic was taking place.*

One day, despondent and despairing, she took the bus into the town centre, unable to face her day at school. As she wandered into the job centre to seek a friend who worked there, she saw the advert that would change her life for ever: an invitation for applications for nurse training. This was an epiphany. An opportunity that offered social distance from her family, safe accommodation, and a professional role with a career pathway. Most of all, she would be able to care for the sick and dying. However, the application required confidence in herself and her abilities. Mary Anne had to overcome nagging thoughts of being worthless. She was also worried about leaving her family to cope without her.

Was Mary Anne always destined for a nursing career? Many years later, when her bedroom was being decorated, her parents found a sketch she had made of Florence Nightingale hidden under the wallpaper. This vocation seemed inevitable. It was not a question of *if*, but *when*.

> *Did I imagine myself being a nurse one day, or was it that I longed for a nurse to care for my wounded soul?*

Intuitive Wisdom

> *Despite my despairing vulnerability, I somehow felt blindly optimistic. Something quite mysterious was conspiring to help me create a better future. I did not feel I needed to be in control. I was neither fearful of the unknown nor afraid to ignore the familiar but was hoping that a journey would emerge, a journey away from this barren landscape into one which was scrupulously fertile. Boldness, patience and determination would accompany me, the teenage wayfarer.*

Trust that you have a silent destiny which is constantly being created. Alchemic magic is taking place.

Your life can unexpectedly change for ever. Your destiny can enter a threshold of profound enlightenment. Your path can take an unprecedented turning towards freedom. Mercy is there for everyone.

> *God does not send us despair in order to kill us; he sends it in order to awaken us to new life.*
> **Hermann Hesse**
> Reflections

Feeling lost and confused can be traded for new goals and inner strength.

If you feel unworthy, with poor self-esteem, be brave and resist these thoughts. Believe in yourself and others will follow.

Do you want to follow the hard road of discipline and reward or the pain of regret and disappointment?

Resilience grows in the face of adversity, chaos and confusion.

Don't give up and don't give in. Keep striving.

Resist imaginings which lead you down a path of misery. Turn your back on dark thoughts and grow in grace.

Refrain from making friends with despair, leaving no room for hope.

> *If only I could resist thoughts of failure and betrayal and listen to my true self. I had a chance to significantly change and improve the circumstances of my life. I could live in a safe and stable place, in a calm atmosphere where I could learn and grow, somewhere I could feel valued and respected. My inner voice encouraged me to try. At least have a go.*

Developing Deeper Consciousness and Taking Compassionate Action

> *My experience in the hotel had served a purpose, showing me the way into nursing, but most of my learning lay hidden beneath the debris at home amid the dreadful human suffering and abuse. Later, throughout my nursing career, I would come to realise how caring for Mum taught me tolerance and compassion, while others offered only prejudice and indifference.*

Can you think of a time when you have cared for someone who is unwell, mentally or physically?

What did you find fulfilling about this experience?

What were the challenges and how did you overcome them?

> *My resilience grew as I surrendered my spirit to this messy, chaotic drama. I resisted enacting my angry impulses. Somehow I still found an inner strength to remain steadfast and calm, despite feeling torn between opposing thoughts of either sudden escape or sticking it out until I had some notion of which way to go.*

What do you understand by the term 'resilience'?

Identify a time in your life when you have felt confident and resilient.

How have your experiences of adversity helped you to become more resilient?

What do you understand by the term 'self-determination'?

Describe a time in your life when you have felt disheartened and demoralised.

What guiding principles and values enabled you to cope?

Can you identify any mat carriers who helped and affirmed you? How did they love, support and guide you?

Think of a time when you have supported others. What success did you achieve?

Chapter 7

An Irreversible Ending
(1980)

Mary Anne had made her decision. She wanted to become a registered nurse. She broke the news to her family as they sat at the dining table. Her mother reacted irrationally, throwing food-covered crockery at her, then violently pulling her hair. Mary Anne refused to retaliate, not through fear, but quiet confidence. She was getting braver and was prepared to defy her parents.

But a second battle was to emerge for Mary Anne. Her inner voice had been made fragile by years of belittlement and ridicule, and this voice tried to tell her she wasn't good enough for nursing and she would fail. However, a new spirit of determination was becoming more powerful within her. She silently told herself: *Not for one moment would I waste my heart on fear anymore.*

She has a nervous and soul-searching interview with Mr Watts, the head of nurse training at the local hospital, in which she was questioned about the impact of her decision on her family. She courageously explained her determination to create an educated future for herself, an act of self-care and self-investment. Her family would have to manage without her. Her application was successful.

Before her training began, Mary Anne felt the need for one more summer working in her seaside Welsh hotel. Her request to defer the start of her training until the autumn was granted. During this last season Mary Anne reflected more deeply on the woman she was becoming. She enjoyed a new sense of freedom and independence as she started to distance herself, both physically and mentally, from her shattered family life.

Mary Anne developed a profound sense of gratitude and love of natural beauty.

> *I had to fulfil this passion, a yearning to be intimate once again with the wild and unpredictable landscape of the coast.*

Intuitive Wisdom

> *It was hard for me to believe I was capable of achieving something good and rewarding. I tried to resist these self-generated accusations. My fragile soul was tormented, but I was going to try. I needed to defy my negative emotions and unhelpful thoughts. My spirit of determination was emerging like a phoenix rising out of the ashes.*

The conscious choice of self-care, which involves prioritising one's wellbeing, precedes caring and supporting others. This requires self-compassion and a deeper self-awareness.

Remember you are capable and you matter.

Sometimes you will need to take risks and trust that God will take care of you. She will guide the flow and destiny of your life.

Refuse to retreat. Instead, confront your inner enemy called 'fear' and allow your spirit of determination to emerge.

There is a choice: the choice of shunning dismal circumstances in exchange for a future of hope and prosperity.

※

Suffering teaches. Indeed, it is an authentic teacher. Caring for someone with an addiction can teach tolerance and compassion.

Avoid a self-imposed spiral of shame.

Surrender to telling the truth. But first you must recognise the truth.

※

Dream of a life filled with love, beauty and purpose.

Learn to feel the wondrous spirit of emancipation.

Developing Deeper Consciousness and Taking Compassionate Action

Despite my fears and dilemmas, I decide to leave home to train as a registered nurse. This decision was fraught with risk and uncertainty.

> *I wouldn't allow my negative self-abasement to manifest itself in destructive behaviours which could sabotage my chances. I was transforming my inner essence into a positive and life-enhancing energy. I was beginning to fly, finding the strength to live the life that I would love. Not for one moment would I waste my heart on fear anymore.*

Identify a time of personal change in your life.

What challenges did you face, and how did you overcome them?

Were there any unintended consequences?

How did others support you through this period of change?

What did you learn about yourself when experiencing this change?

How would you support someone going through a period of change?

> *A self that goes on changing is a self that goes on living.*
> **Virginia Woolf**

Can you recall being aware of negative self-talk, such as 'I am a failure', 'I am stupid', 'I will fail', 'I am not good enough'?

Were you able to resist these thoughts? If so, how? If you were unable to resist negative self-talk, what was stopping you?

Are you aware of what triggers any self-limiting beliefs and what can you do to avoid them?

What can you do about these self-limiting beliefs so you can adopt a more positive and confident self-image?

Who can support you by affirming and validating you?

> *During my quieter moments, I had a deeper sense of who I was becoming: a young woman who was growing away from a shattered family towards a future of hope and optimism. I was beginning to feel the wondrous spirit of emancipation as I spent warm sunny afternoons on the beach in deep conversation with myself. I began to imagine how good my life could be.*

Chapter 8

The Call of the Nightingale
(1980 – 1983)

Mary Anne began nurse training. The calm, soothing atmosphere of the hospital accommodation away from her family was music to her soul.

Other changes were happening within the family. Lee moved to the south coast to join the Royal Navy. Mum admitted herself full time into an addiction clinic, which enabled her to withdraw from her alcohol dependency.

> *Mum had willingly surrendered her shrewish character for a journey of tender healing. What gave her courage to withstand the agony of withdrawal from her crutch whisky? It was love. Loving care crept into her life from the kindness of strangers.*

Dad had taken a less demanding role at work and was more relaxed without the responsibility of two teenagers at home. But, despite these changes and improvements, Mary Anne still mistrusted her mother after experiencing years of lies, deceit and betrayal.

She continued to wrestle with poor self-esteem and feelings of not being good enough, an imposter. But her true self, her true soul, pushed through the doubt to reassure her that she was capable and worthy of her position as a student nurse. She was determined to succeed.

Her newfound emancipation from the tyranny of her family and enrolment into a respectable profession generated a fear of loss. Mary Anne now had something to lose, something precious. She realised she had to grow in maturity and apply herself to her training programme, to gracefully accept the rigorous discipline, rules and protocols, if she was to achieve her dream of becoming a fully qualified and socially independent professional.

Mary Anne's young and ambitious tutor, Miss Jenkins, summoned Mary Anne to her office and told her to change her aloof attitude. Mary Anne realised her reserve was a defence mechanism, developed over years of abuse and ridicule to shield her battered self-esteem. She reassessed her attitude towards others. Without challenge, she apologised and promised to change. She became a model student, passing her exams and assessments with flying colours, a true ambassador for the nursing profession.

Part way through Mary Anne's training programme, she became consumed with anxiety for her brother. War had broken out in the Falkland Islands and Lee's ship had been called to duty in the South Atlantic. At seventeen, Lee was barely an adult. She also feared their mother would return to her alcohol addiction, unable to cope with the stress of the war.

After the conflict, Lee returned home to a hero's welcome. Mum had remained sober. Could this be a new era for the family? Certainly Mary Anne was cautiously willing to forgive past wrongs.

Intuitive Wisdom

> *The career I had embarked on would demand strength and resilience. The witnessing of human pain, sorrow and loss would often leave me feeling agonisingly helpless. When dealing with the many forms of human suffering I would be utterly wretched and bereft at the absence of meaning.*

Caring for the sick and dying is emotionally and physically demanding and requires great resolve.

Sometimes it is necessary to conform to authority and discipline.

Listen with your heart, first to understand then to be understood. Avoid critical assumptions.

There is part of us known to others and not known to ourselves. When this is revealed to us, we should use the information to cultivate growth and wisdom.

Resist that which you cannot change and grow in resilience.

Learn to be humble.

※

Diligence and determination can create distance from failure and take you closer to your desired goals.

Believe in and live your authentic passion. This can be life giving and life enhancing, enabling you to thrive and reach your true potential.

※

Sometimes it is only by grace that we can forgive what is not necessarily a conscious act.

> *An invisible benevolence was emerging from within me, carrying me towards a loving light full of radiant hope and new beginnings.*

Developing Deeper Consciousness and Taking Compassionate Action

> *I became doubtful and gloomy about my ability to succeed at my nurse training. Had I been taking refuge in my own fantasies, fooling myself I was clever enough? Tormented by the memory of the acidic comments so often claimed as truths by my teachers, I began to believe I was an imposter. Perhaps I was only offered a place out of pity because I had shared information about my family. I began to sabotage my own success. I wasn't intelligent enough, and neither was I worthy of something good happening to me. Only bad things happened in my life; it was all my fault. I was the one to blame. I was about to commence my nurse training convinced I was a fraud.*

Describe your understanding of imposter syndrome.

Reflect on your life experience to identify if you have ever experienced this.

If so, why do you think you may be vulnerable to this syndrome?

What steps can you take to overcome it in the future?

What support and guidance will you need?

※

Describe the first day of one of your most significant life-changing choices, such as the day you started paid work or university.

Did you have any inkling that your life was about to be defined by this, that you were crossing a threshold?

What did you learn about yourself during such planned change?

What effect did this life-enhancing transition have on those close to you, such as your partner, family and friends?

How do these memories inspire you today?

How does your experience of planned change compare to change you have experienced that was unplanned?

※

In this chapter I am faced with an accusation that I was standoffish and had an attitude problem.

> *I was startled by her remark, but I realised I had to respond in a way which was pleasing to her, despite wanting to contest the validity of her allegation. What I really wanted to say was: 'No, no. Please understand me. You're wrong. I'm not behaving badly. It's my way of coping in a world where I feel threatened. This is how I survive. I'm not standoffish, I'm sensitive and nervous in company, especially with large groups of girls.' Until this moment I had little awareness of how others saw me.*

Can you describe a situation when you became aware of how others saw you, which was different to your self-perception?

Were you able to use this information as an opportunity for personal growth and to learn more about yourself? Or were you defensive and dismissive?

How do you think your partner, family, friends and colleagues would describe you?

How does this compare to your self-perception?

Chapter 9

Carpe Diem
(1983 – 1984)

Mary Anne completed her nurse training and qualified as a Registered General Nurse, achieving her first professional milestone. She started work on a surgical ward in the hospital where she did her training. Enthusiastic and eager to keep learning, she quickly became disillusioned and frustrated by the parochialism of her nursing colleagues and their out-of-date custom and practices.

> *I was offered a short-term contract as a staff nurse on a 30-bed female surgical ward. During my training this had been one of three areas I had found lacking in acceptable standards of care. Needless to say, my observations had made me unpopular.*

Listening and trusting her inner voice, Mary Anne realised she needed to move away from the impoverished industrialised region where she lived and find a place with less deprivation and hardship. She was beginning to understand that her soul was longing to live in a place of quiet beauty surrounded by nature in order to thrive and prosper. But where?

She decided to move to Cambridge to work at the new Addenbrooke's teaching hospital. It was fewer than two hundred miles south, but light years away from where she had grown up. It was a place of gentle beauty and green spaces, cosmopolitan and cultured.

> *I was told strange stories about this faraway land: privileged people punting down the River Cam, May balls, debutantes in silk taffeta gowns, aristocrats, pink champagne, swarms of bicycles, and dons in swirling academic robes.*

When she arrived in Cambridge she worried about being an imposter, an outsider. She felt awkward and conscious of her northern working class accent. But she quickly fell in love with the place – its charm, the architecture, the diversity of people and the dignity and mutual respect in which they lived. It was romantic and awe-inspiring.

A couple of months after she arrived, Mary Anne experienced the sudden and traumatic death of a fellow staff nurse who lived in the room next door in the nurses' home. She had known that Debbie was troubled by an undisclosed problem. That day they had been out for lunch and Debbie had drunk heavily. Later that evening Mary Anne had visited her room to check how she was feeling only to find her lifeless on her bed. It emerged that Debbie was a lesbian and that a former lover had been blackmailing her. The local newspapers turned the story into a cheap scandal, splashing headlines about Debbie's sexuality: *Gay Nurse Dies After Heavy Drinking Session.*

> Debbie's vulnerable short life was shamelessly paraded to sell more newspapers.

This painful tragedy deepened Mary Anne's awareness of the beauty and fragility of life.

> *Once again in my life I was saved by beauty – the beauty of nature as well as of music. My senses were the threshold to the preservation of my soul; they allowed invisible miracles to take place. Nature and music were my mat carriers, restoring my spirit so that I could carry on despite what had happened.*

Intuitive Wisdom

> *Power struggles prevailed in an atmosphere of stale custom and ritualistic practice. The ward sister was lazy, forgetful and incapable of leading her ship of fools. Rather than challenging her, the ward staff colluded with her to protect themselves and the status quo.*

Avoid colluding with outmoded methods, laziness, stale custom and ritualistic practice. Strive for excellence.

Always search for improvement. Never compromise your integrity.

Find the courage to challenge the status quo, fixed opinions and parochial attitudes.

Avoid and ignore petty gossip. It can ruin morale, trust, respect and commitment.

※

Learn to respond to suffering, especially the suffering of victims of violence, abuse, prejudice, discrimination and injustice, with love.

Discover the power of compassion.

※

> *They taunted and jeered the other passengers. Vulgar, threatening language combined with spitting and flicking nose pickings entertained their troubled souls. I can't do this, I can't live with this, I silently screamed. I need peaceful beauty and fragrant tranquillity, not this vile intimidation. I knew I had to make a decision about the course my life would take.*

All feelings carry messages and insights into our interior world. Melancholy and frustration as well as happiness and joy tell us more than we already know.

Step out of your boat onto the sea of uncertainty, trusting you will not drown. A life-changing threshold full of adventure awaits you.

When you make a commitment you will find an inner strength to inspire and enable you to fulfil your destiny.

Trust your gut feeling – your intuition – even if it means disagreement and conflict with others.

Always be aware that the media are shamelessly capable of parading lies, untruths and human vulnerability for commercial benefit.

Some prefer to be self-satisfied and comfortable with media untruths rather than accepting the discomfort of the full truth.

> *I was touched by the vivid beauty of life: strangers offering a quiet 'good morning', a faint smile from an innocent, shy child, and the bright yellow glow from endless fields of flowering rapeseed. The very act of living felt more precious, intense and glorious.*

Following a period of trauma, sadness or suffering, our senses can reawaken to the natural beauty around us. What may previously have gone unnoticed is now more visible and beautiful. We are blessed by surprising luminous moments and we feel more alive.

> *Beauty Beckons*
> *When beauty beckons*
> *We see more clearly*
> *Feel more deeply and*
> *Love more generously*

Developing Deeper Consciousness and Taking Compassionate Action

> *Frustrated and disillusioned, I could not escape the thought that there had to be a better way of doing things. Perhaps it was time to leave behind that which I had outgrown, in pursuit of my true life's desires. I had to get away. Not by fleeing in terror and confusion like some tortured migrant, but with thoughtful planning and exploration. I became the lonely seeker in search of a place where I could belong and flourish.*

Describe what you understand by *carpe diem*.

How does this concept influence your life?

❦

What personal qualities do you need to challenge or avoid those who gossip, engage in petty conversation or are overly critical and condemnatory?

❦

What are the challenges when caring for those who are suffering?

How do you respond to suffering? How would you prefer to respond?

Reflect on the harm we can do to ourselves when we miss an opportunity to offer compassion to ourselves and those who are suffering.

What actions can you take to improve your ability to help those who suffer?

❦

Describe a situation when you have felt in need of advice because you were vulnerable.

Who would you trust for guidance and support?

What do you understand by 'a person of integrity'? Are people with integrity born or made?

❦

> *Louise told me she'd had a long intimate chat with Debbie about her problems after I had left the pub to go shopping, but she didn't go into details as Debbie had asked her not to. I suggested we tell the home warden and ask her to check on Debbie later, but Louise didn't want to involve anyone else. She was uncompromising, firmly stating that it was no one else's business. This didn't make sense to me. Why couldn't we ask for support? Louise was older*

> *than me with a more senior nursing position. I felt that she was asserting her professional authority and I passively submitted. I didn't listen to my own inner voice. I gave away my own personal power.*

This incident describes how I was weakened by someone else's seniority and confident ability to assert their views and opinions over mine.

Can you identify a situation when you believe you, too, were unable to express your views and opinions?

What would you do differently another time?

What would you do differently another time?

How do you see society's acceptance of the LGBTQ community changing?

How can we improve our support for the LGBTQ community?

What actions can you take to improve people's perceptions of gender identity, sexuality, stigma (public and self), injustice and discrimination?

> *The coroner concluded it was a sudden unexplained adult death, an adult cot death. The story was turned into a cheap scandal, splashed across the front page of the local press: Gay Nurse Dies After Heavy Drinking Session. Debbie's vulnerable short life was shamelessly paraded to sell more newspapers.*

Do you agree that the media are shamelessly capable of parading lies, untruths and human vulnerability for commercial benefit?

Chapter 10

Pride and Prestige
(1984 – 1989)

Mary Anne's career flourished and she qualified for numerous nursing specialisms. She was driven by her desire to learn and prosper, but she was also fearful of sliding backwards into the life she had distanced herself from.

Despite her career progression, she was still tormented by feelings of worthlessness and low self-esteem. She tried to resolve this by working and studying harder, to the detriment of her social life and taking holidays.

> *I wasn't good enough, so I had to keep improving myself. It was too risky to settle for the status quo; just living my life was not enough. I would later discover I was struggling with imposter syndrome: an inability to believe in one's own achievements and a fear of being exposed as a fraud.*

She moved to Papworth, another hospital in Cambridge and one of the most prestigious medical institutions in the world, renowned for ground-breaking cardiothoracic surgery, medicine and research. She met high-profile visitors and worked alongside some of the world's best medical professionals.

> *Its culture dynamic and transformational, it was a magnet for an international workforce, and people would travel from the other side of the world to work there. I was excited and thrived on an atmosphere of exemplary clinical practice, working beside some of the world's best surgeons, nurses, physiotherapists and pharmacists. I met princesses and politicians, dukes and prime ministers.*

But Mary Anne clashed with her manager, a bully with a facade of easy charm, who used blame to deflect any criticism onto others while deftly accepting praise for successes she had little to do with. Feeling threatened, Mary Anne took a new post in a neighbouring hospital as a nurse teacher.

Then Mary Anne's best friend introduced her to Andrew, a close friend of her brother. Andrew immediately wanted a serious relationship, but Mary Anne wasn't sure about him. She was confused and emotionally ill-equipped to cope with an intimate relationship.

> I began to subjugate my own needs to Andrew's. Such self-sacrifice assuaged the guilt I sometimes felt about the life I had been living as a single woman, a life with my personal freedom at the heart of it.

In the absence of trustworthy loving relationships in her life to guide her she ignored her instincts and allowed herself to become involved with him. She had little emotional background to draw upon. Most of her experiences with men to this point had been negative: being taking advantage of and exploited.

After dating for a while Mary Anne and Andrew went on holiday and Andrew asked her to marry him. Part of her was delighted that someone cared enough about her to suggest marriage. She tried hard to convince herself that this was a normal and natural part of life. After all, most of her friends were now married and having children. Why shouldn't she?

Plans were made and both sets of parents got excited about the prospect of a wedding.

> An invisible force was sweeping me along. My feet were no longer on solid ground. I had slipped off the shore and like a piece of driftwood was floating in the sea. Carried along by the current, I lacked the self-awareness and self-esteem I needed to get back onto dry land. I ignored my inner wisdom. I was powerless to resist.

Meanwhile, Mary Anne's inner voice was telling her something very different. She had doubts. Andrew had shown himself to be obsessive, particularly with diet and exercise. Mary Anne was uncertain about the road she was being pulled down but kept quiet, too afraid to disappoint others. In her mind, 'It would all be my fault, as usual' if anything went wrong.

Three months before they were due to be married, Mary Anne called the wedding off. She blamed her own inadequacies for the decision, to alleviate the guilt she felt.

> *I deliberately made myself the scapegoat to alleviate my guilt for inducing disappointment and anger. I used victimhood to my advantage. It was self-preservation.*

Intuitive Wisdom

> *I had to model the behaviour I expected from others; I could not project my misery onto them. I had to turn my distress into inspirational optimism and positive encouragement.*

When faced with adversity, trust your own efforts and persevere; you deserve success, prosperity and peace.

Remember to balance self-improvement with self-care and self-compassion.

Make time for the ordinary things in life which evoke a sense of pleasure and enjoyment, such as a walk in the countryside, time with friends or sitting by a lake watching wildlife.

> *In the sweetness of friendship let there be laughter, and sharing of pleasures. For in the dew of little things, the heart finds its morning and is refreshed.*
> **Kahlil Gibran**
> The Prophet

Seek out compassionate cultures free from shame, blame, judgement or condemnation.

Belonging to a caring community will enable you to thrive and reach your true potential.

A restless spirit can carry you to new places of self-discovery and adventure.

> *I was struggling with my boss who was micromanaging me. She had an excessive almost neurotic need to control and check my work. She obsessively inspected and monitored every detail in search of fault and imperfection. The atmosphere was one of suspicion and mistrust.*

Bullying is insulting, intimidating and malicious and arrives in many shapes and sizes. There is the overt bully, the loud, openly aggressive person who terrorises employees. And there is the covert bully, who quietly disrupts, threatens, isolates, confuses, and causes anxiety and unrest.

A leader's effectiveness can be significantly influenced by how we perceive them – for better or worse. It is a social construct crafted through a narrative and images of a desired future.

Avoid those who have a tendency to be hurtful and negative by complaining and criticising.

The graceful invitation of beauty will deepen your self-knowledge and growth by touching those parts deep within that you are yet to fully understand. Your very essence will be transformed as you discover fresh hope and inspiration.

When preparing for marriage, the enthusiasm of family and friends can engulf and subjugate your ability to cancel or postpone the wedding despite your grave concerns.

False illusions of lifelong marital happiness and security can be born from exaggerated emotions of excitement.

Emotional regulation when making a lifelong decision such as marriage is an imperative.

Developing Deeper Consciousness and Taking Compassionate Action

Identify a leader you admire. What qualities make them successful?

Now identify someone you think is an ineffective leader. What characteristics do they display?

◆◇◆

How would you define a bully?

Why do you think adults and children bully others?

If you have been a victim of bullying, describe what effect this had on you.

Were you able to challenge the bully? If not, what prevented you?

What would you advise someone to do if they were being bullied?

◆◇◆

> *Periods of solitude were essential to me. Long walks alone in places of divine beauty brought emotional recovery and refreshment from the demands of nursing the sick and dying. A calm found only in the company of nature would slow my racing thoughts and hectic heart, uncluttering my mind and allowing me to find acceptance of the harshness of suffering.*

Describe what you do to cope with everyday pressures and demands.

After reading this chapter, is there anything you would like to do differently to cope with times when you feel under pressure?

◆◇◆

> *Both our families were instantly engulfed in wedding plans, creating an illusion of happiness and security, enabling us to avoid uncovering any*

> *emotional secrets which lay beneath the surface. Dress codes, flowers, hymns, rings, confetti, invitations, speeches and menus distracted all of us from asking if we were truly compatible. The vicar agreed to marry us after one brief administrative meeting. There was not a single probing word and no curiosity about our motives and values.*

Can you think of a time when you deceived yourself to avoid dealing with a difficult situation?

How could you have approached this differently to minimise a harmful outcome?

How would you react to advice and guidance which is uncomfortable and challenging?

What would you say to a friend in a similar situation?

Chapter 11

The Prelude to Illumination
(1989 – 1991)

Andrew was contrite and blamed himself for the collapse of the relationship. Mary Anne listened and believed he was truly remorseful. They got married. Some might think this foolish, but Mary Anne had an overwhelming need to be loved and she had no great understanding of what a caring relationship should feel like. She invested her hopeful heart in Andrew.

Once married, it became all too obvious that this relationship would be physically and psychologically abusive. Mary Anne was thrust once again into emotional turmoil. Andrew was lazy, making no effort to help with domestic chores. He spent money he didn't have, which caused financial problems. He was often drunk and acted as if Mary Anne were his personal property. He was verbally and sexually abusive and obsessed with body image.

Mary Anne has been blessed with physical attractiveness, but this can equally be a curse. Are her good looks the motivation behind men's interest in her? She realised Andrew wanted an attractive but compliant wife who did as she was told. He wasn't interested in Mary Anne as a person. Her needs and wellbeing were disregarded.

Mary Anne's first notion was to submit and try to make the marriage work, but it soon became apparent that her efforts would be fruitless. Andrew was obsessive, paranoid and addicted to alcohol. He ignored her attempts to get him to seek help. After two years of suffering his abusive and unpredictable behaviour, she left him and took refuge in a nurse's residence.

She received no compassion or understanding from either her mother or her mother-in-law. Both felt it was her duty to endure an unhappy marriage as they had done themselves. Mary Anne felt enormous guilt and shame.

Once again she found a way forward through immersing herself in education. This included a course in person-centred counselling, which proved to be a revelation. She began to understand her true self with a new clarity and insight.

> *I embarked on training to teach adults and complemented this with a part-time counselling course. I wanted to understand the human condition more deeply. I was curious and mystified about human behaviour and emotions, especially my own. I wanted to relate to people with greater authenticity and compassion. Like a still silent dawn, I began to awaken to my true self.*

The Gulf War broke out and Lee was sent into action. Mary Anne was once more consumed by anxiety for her brother.

> *This style of warfare was different. His previous encounter with the horrors of war consisted of guns, bullets and missiles. Gulf War armed forces were exposed to a unique mix of hazards not previously experienced during wartime. There were neurotoxins, such as the nerve gas sarin, the anti-nerve gas drug pyridostigmine bromide, and pesticides that affect the nervous system. The oil and smoke that spewed from hundreds of burning oil wells presented another hazard.*

On his return from his tour of duty, in a highly unusual move, Lee reached out to her; she had had very little contact with him over many years. Lee confided in her that he had suicidal thoughts. He was suffering with complex PTSD. Mary Anne took on the role of big sister and protector. Desperate to find help, she eventually phoned the chaplain aboard Lee's ship – 'Paddy the Padre'. It was a phone call that would change the course of Mary Anne's life.

Intuitive Wisdom

> *My soul was screaming with rage, but my childhood abuse meant I lacked the courage I needed to speak out. Feelings of shame and worthlessness*

> *robbed my voice. Somehow I deserved this. I'd been foolish enough to trust him – to marry him. I suffered silently, certain that no one would believe me if I told them what was going on. I couldn't even tell my closest friends.*

Children and adults with a history of abuse can develop a strong sense of loyalty towards their abuser, despite the fact that the bond is damaging to them.

Once married, the abuser feels safe in the knowledge they have trapped you. The abuse may be insidious and subtle, beginning with put-downs and disrespect, but then may grow into physical abuse.

Pay attention to the warning signs of a relationship becoming harmful, even though it may feel uncomfortable and disappointing. It is natural to want the relationship to succeed and so deny any mistreatment.

> *I vividly remember him stating that I was now his wife and he could behave as he liked. He was not going to be a doormat. It was a great victory for him. When we married, his pursuit of me came to an end. He had conquered me, and his supremacy over me would reign. I had become legally his.*

Fear and anxiety, perhaps experienced through humiliation and punishment, can warn us of harmful people and circumstances but can also block our senses so that we become alienated from our true feelings. We can become paralysed by this negativity.

Try to discern that which seeks to warn and protect you. Sometimes fear and apprehension are signals alerting you to situations that require greater skill, wisdom and effort. These emotions are also capable of teaching you more about yourself so that you may find greater meaning, purpose and fulfilment.

Listen to the abiding wisdom deep within you.

Despite the darkness, there is always a horizon illuminated by hope.

You won't become a bad person because bad things have happened to you.

Avoid blaming yourself. Self-protection is an imperative.

Strive against adversity. Emotional endurance and wilful determination in the face of fear and anxiety will not be wasted. These will enable you to grow in strength and resilience, which will sustain and protect you throughout your life.

> *I may not have had the sense to resist marrying him, but I did have the sense to stay alive. I vowed Andrew would not be the author of my decline, emotionally or physically. My life experiences of striving against adversity were sustaining and protecting me from becoming encumbered by further permanent affliction.*

Anticipatory grief, such as when a loved one goes to fight in a war, is a complex dynamic process. A heightened concern and preparation for dying can manifest as part of the grieving process. Anxiety, guilt, denial, depression, anger and bargaining with God for an alternative and more desirable outcome can be experienced prior to the imagined loss.

Caring for a loved one with PTSD can be overwhelming and specialised professional support is needed. This disorder can be complex and may require such help over a long period of time.

Skilled support for someone suffering from PTSD may prevent them using unhealthy coping mechanisms such as drugs and or alcohol.

> *Silenced by the gravity of his suffering I wept as I held him in the stillness beneath the milky moonlight. Lee was suffering from PTSD – post-traumatic stress disorder. The trauma caused by the*

> *Gulf War far exceeded the ordinary vicissitudes of life such as illness and financial hardship. Lee was overwhelmed, and the effects were catastrophic.*

Listen and love with a tender heart.

Developing Deeper Consciousness and Taking Compassionate Action

> *How do you know you can spend the rest of your life married to the same person? Isn't this the promise we make when we decide to get married? Can you ever know or is it blind faith? Are we equipped with sufficient knowledge and experience to make such profound promises?*

Think of a relationship or friendship in which you experienced disappointment.

What effect did this have on you: your thoughts, feelings, behaviour and mood?

Were you able to resolve this with the person who disappointed you?

Is there something you would like to say or do differently next time?

†⌒†

Think of someone known to you who is struggling with their mental health.

How does this affect you?

How do you show them compassion?

†⌒†

What do you see as the myths and stigma around mental health?

If you have had counselling, what did you gain from
the experience?

Would you recommend it to a friend/loved one in need?

Can you think of any individuals who are breaking the barriers
and inspiring freedom from the misconceptions and stigma
associated with mental health difficulties?

Describe the extent to which you own responsibility for your
thoughts, feelings and behaviour.

What personal qualities are needed to take responsibility in
this way?

Do you feel you have a tendency to attribute too much
responsibility to yourself (self-blame) or too little (avoidance)?

Can you identify someone who has changed the course of your life
for the better?

Do you think they are aware of the impact they have had on you?

What would you like to say to them?

What effect might it have on them, once they are aware?

Chapter 12

Priests, Ships and Hounds
(1991 – 1994)

Mary Anne had a lengthy phone call with Paddy the Padre to discuss Lee's welfare. Towards the end of the call he took her by surprise when he asked: 'And what about you?' Mary Anne was struck by the chaplain's empathy and caring enquiry. The question lingered.

> *There were no interruptions as he let me talk. He did not need to satisfy his own curiosity nor dominate our conversation with his ego. He listened so that I had a quiet space to think, compose and tell my story. He seemed comfortable with silence. It was as though I was sitting next to him in the same room. I could feel his non-judgemental, celestial presence. This was my first knowing encounter with the grace of God; I was walking on holy ground and my soul knew it.*

Having secured support for Lee, Mary Anne now had to deal with the repercussions of her divorce from Andrew. She walked away from the marriage with only her personal possessions, anxious to make a clean break and unable to cope with lengthy legal negotiations. She visited their former home one last time and was shocked to find Andrew had created a shrine to her in the living room, full of enlarged photographic portraits. Andrew would stalk Mary Anne for many years.

Increasingly, Mary Anne was drawn to sacred spaces: churches and cathedrals. She sensed God was entering her life. She became preoccupied by the spiritual and mystical.

> *I had been running through the dark labyrinth of my life ever since I could remember, breathlessly*

> *searching for peace and love, but looking in all the wrong places.*

Mary Anne willingly opened herself up to a new way of being. Self-loathing and self-condemnation still followed her, but she knew these were the wounds of her childhood experiences. The difference now was that an inner voice was telling her she would recover from this harm, but the healing journey may be long, arduous and painful.

She understood that she could no longer live a life defined by past abuse.

> *I didn't spot the pothole in the road. I was an emotional mess. My interior landscape was like one of the abandoned industrial sites I had left behind in my hometown.*

She hid herself away in her cottage in a new village and decided to go into long-term psychodynamic therapy. The process was exhausting and took almost three years, dredging up past hurts, abuse and neglect. In this safe place of peace and trust, Mary Anne was keen to unpack the inner rubble of her life in the hope that she would find a better future free from the misery of her past hurts. Martha, her therapist, encouraged her to read Christian books, which she did eagerly.

On 3 April 1994, Easter Sunday, Mary Anne made her commitment to God. She visualised God as a loving, nurturing female figure rather than a male, perhaps because much of her experience of the masculine thus far had been of exploitation and abuse.

Changes in her life were subtle but significant. She became calmer and began to experience an inner peace. Her therapy combined with her newfound faith brought a feeling of physical and psychological safety. She likened finding God to a homecoming. This spiritual enlightenment changed her life forever.

> *I sensed an inner transformation of sweet gratitude and meekness. Like a child, without question I trusted the grace of God could set me free from all my past hurts. I was slowly admitting my deepest desire: to receive and offer genuine love. It was an enlightenment that would change me forever.*

Intuitive Wisdom

> *I uncovered many unresolved issues buried deep within my wounded soul which had distorted my authentic self. It was as if my life had been a journey along a dimly lit corridor of sticky cobwebs and damaged mirrors, trapping me with false images. Until then I had believed the lies of those reflections. For the first time in my life I was able to externalise repressed emotions, such as anger, shame, guilt and sadness.*

We perpetuate our own suffering by refusing to relinquish our attachment to people, possessions and positions which are not in our best interests. Detach yourself from that which does not serve you well.

The path of psychotherapy and journaling has many possibilities, all of which journey toward greater access to your unconscious, allowing you to discover important hidden insights. This leads to wisdom and wholeness.

Negative self-images projected by those who stigmatise and discriminate against you can be transformed by finding new images for yourself which empower and revitalise you. There is freedom from shame and humiliation as you discover life-enhancing ways to see the world around you.

Discover and accept the truth about your unique childhood history, no matter how uncomfortable or unpleasant this can be.

You are not defined by a history mottled by suffering, abuse and harmful relationships.

Your therapist is like a wise guide in the wilderness. Don't forget they too may have faced their own hurts, pain and struggles – 'the wounded healer'.

Increased self-awareness gained from psychotherapy will enable you to be more empathetic towards others. This can deepen your personal relationships.

Search for your true self, freedom from past hurts, healing, beauty, love and soulful equanimity.

> *A small grain of wisdom was encouraging me to persevere. Despite the absence of hope and the pervading uncertainty of my life, I sensed I must travel this vocational journey.*

Vulnerability is not a failure. It is a deep sensitivity to feeling unsafe, defenceless and exposed. It is an innate part of the human condition.

As we embrace our vulnerability we discover our shared humanity, courage and hope.

Strive to heal and transform yourself into a stronger, wiser human being. It's not about where you are going but who you are becoming that matters.

> *I had to do something. I had to abandon harmful and destructive habits. I couldn't continue as I was. I couldn't live with an identity defined by past and present abuse. I had to let go and transform the pain and suffering into wisdom and new life.*

Inside your heart there are secret sources of courage. Search and claim these. Then you will find the strength to abandon harmful and destructive habits and relationships.

If God is personified, then God can be 'she' rather than 'he', a creative feminine nurturer breathing life into all things, a God who is tender, gracious, steadfast and faithful. Female images of God move away from authority, dominance and patriarchy.

Faith is a different kind of knowing. It brings greater inner authority than rational knowing. This will humble you.

Deepen your consciousness through contemplative prayer. This daily practice of deep listening helps us connect with divine love.

Developing Deeper Consciousness and Taking Compassionate Action

> *I had normalised the abnormal. As a consequence, I didn't hear the warning bells about Andrew.*

Can you describe a situation in your life when you have normalised the abnormal, such as maintaining a friendship with someone who constantly lies to you and lets you down.

Why do you think you allowed this situation to develop?

What would you like to do differently if this was to happen again?

※

If someone close to you was unhappily married, what advice and support could you offer?

What do you see as the barriers to someone seeking marital guidance?

※

> *With an unhurried and unperturbed pace, God followed my fleeing soul by her divine grace.*

Reflect on the presence of God in your life.

Can you list some of your beliefs about God? 'God is goodness', for example.

Do your beliefs about God include 'We are all made in the image of God'?

What can you share with others about how God manifests in your life?

How would you describe God to a child?

※

I fled Him, down the nights and down the days;
  I fled Him, down the arches of the years;
I fled Him, down the labyrinthine ways
  Of my own mind; and in the midst of tears
I hid from Him, and under running laughter.
    Up vistaed hopes I sped; And shot, precipitated,
Adown Titanic glooms of chasmed fears,
  From those strong Feet that followed,
followed after.

Francis Thompson
The Hound of Heaven

Chapter 13

Paradox and Paranoia
(1994 – 1996)

As Mary Anne's faith grew, she became calmer and happier. She formed new friendships with people who were at peace with themselves: gentle and honest women with ascetic lifestyles like her own. These become her kindred spirits.

> *My focus was shifting from the heroic to the transformative, from acquisition to giving, and from achieving to serving.*

As Mary Anne began her journey of faith and healing, the emotional and psychological distance from her family was increasing, which felt natural and inevitable for everyone.

> *Lee and his wife were convinced I had become an eccentric religious nut and had joined a cult. Dad refused to discuss anything to do with faith and the church; he was uncertain about the existence of God. Mum hid her faith. She was a closet believer, tormented by her Catholic guilt.*

Through therapy Mary Anne's self-awareness deepened and she was reminded that no-one is immune from suffering. Each of us at some stage in our lives will suffer; lives can be filled with disillusionment and disappointment. But she also learned that suffering can be a way to truly grow as a person.

Lee was now voluntarily discharged from the navy. His abuse of alcohol was increasing, as was his bad behaviour. Mary Anne paid him a visit. Early one evening, in a drunken state, without provocation, he lashed out at her and she was traumatised by his irrational rage.

> *The abusive typhoon tore through me leaving a trail of emotional devastation.*

Despite all her efforts over the years to protect and care for her younger brother, he was aggressive and hostile towards her. This tirade reminded Mary Anne of her mother's violent drunken outbursts, which had terrified her. She sat frozen, unable to cope with Lee's uncontrollable emotional state. Intimidated, Mary Anne avoided seeing her brother from this point forward.

Aside from the family dramas, Mary Anne's life was becoming harmonious and balanced. Work was interesting, challenging and intellectually stimulating. She had an inspiring leader, Mary, who enabled her to continue to grow professionally. A circle of close, loving and trusted friends brought some compensation for past hurts.

One day Mary Anne received a call from the hospital reception. It was Andrew, and he wanted to see her. She knew he was stalking her, cycling long distances to try to find out where she was living, but to ask to see her was out of the ordinary. With calm confidence she met him. She was shocked by what she saw. He was emaciated, almost skeletal, and paranoid. Mary Anne expressed her concern over his mental state and Andrew, perhaps for the first time, admitted to his problems. He asked Mary Anne where he could seek help. She pointed him to the British Association of Counsellors and his GP. She never saw him again.

Intuitive Wisdom

> *It was plain to see a radiant springtime was blossoming in my heart. Gloomy clouds of sadness and doubt were being chased away by this hound of heaven. I was discovering a new clarity, peace and happiness.*

The response to your newfound faith and spirituality may surprise and disappoint you. Your transcendental delight may provoke prejudicial fear in others. This can manifest as silent denial, anger and hurtful labelling.

You may become the target of false accusations which are like projected arrows aimed at wounding you to protect the ego of the spiritual sceptic.

> Lee and Karen were adamant there was no God. Their lives were godless and angry. If there was a God then there was hell: Lee had been there. The legacy of his experiences of war bleached any sense of spirituality from their conscious being. He held these views with concrete certainty. He was scarred by the viciousness of humanity.

Do not assume the closeness of family links means you cannot be harmed by those nearest to you.

Try to abandon harmful relationships, even if these involve family members. Focus on your wellbeing by concentrating on ways of self-care and self-compassion.

Unattended mental illness blended with alcohol abuse is a destructive cocktail. Like throwing an incendiary device, relationships can suddenly burst into flames and become permanently ruined, leaving only a legacy of ash and debris.

> Then, unprovoked, Lee betrayed me. If there had been any bonding between us, it was now destroyed. He exploded with an unflinching hatred I had not witnessed before. Sitting opposite me at the dining table he spewed out a series of horrid accusations. As I heard him call me a 'lefty feminist bitch' I froze in merciful deafness. I could see him but my senses protected me by silencing him. It was like watching a frenzied Alfred Hitchcock film with the sound turned off.

When living a life of faith seek out others who are spiritually aware, who adopt a more ascetic lifestyle with a natural soulful shyness, whose natures are compassionate and unassuming.

Spend time with those who radiate unaffected authenticity, living a sacred life.

There is an appealing collective solidarity amongst people of faith in these times of ego-driven greed, consumerism and individualism. Their quiet lives don't need brash boasting and feelings of superiority to those around them.

Those who are faithful to the sacred try to resist being driven by their egos, choosing instead a life of creative service with peaceful and loving hearts.

> *He who dwells in friendship dwells in God, and God in him. The fountain and source of friendship is love, there can be love without friendship, but friendship without love is impossible.*
> **Aelred of Rievaulx**
> Spiritual Friendship

It takes courage and sacrificial faith to shed the false faces of self-deception, collusion with conformity, loveless thoughts and unkind acts for the pursuit of your truest being.

> *To thine own self be true, and it must follow, as the night the day, thou canst not then be false to any man.*
> **William Shakespeare**
> Hamlet Act 1, Scene 3

Turn your back on status, materialism and financial greed. Choose instead to gracefully nurture your soul through the mess, mystery and magic of life by becoming more socially focused, unconditionally loving, respectful of natural beauty, wildlife and the natural world.

> *My soul was being beckoned from the prison of my self-limiting beliefs to the freedom of God's wonder, marvel and awe. An unnameable ache deep in my soul had been forgotten. I had rejected its call for a life of compromise and false promises of safety and*

> *security. Like a window being flung open to fresh morning sunlight, a holy and life-giving spirit had entered in. The voice of the sacred could be heard and I was responding.*

Discover deep unlived parts of who you are so that you may thrive.

Pursue activities such as reading, journaling and meditation, which seek to deepen your self-awareness and aid your search for patterns of meaning and wisdom.

Remember, we all will suffer at some point in their lives and that this can be a way to truly grow as a person.

Create a rhythm with your own unique nature so that life will flow and balance naturally.

Light is always stronger than darkness. The deeper the darkness, the brighter the light.

> *Mary's leadership enabled me to excel locally and nationally. She was my mat carrier. With her trust and respect, my self-confidence came alive. Deep unlived parts of my personality and capability thrived. I was in rhythm with my own unique nature as my life flowed and balanced naturally.*

Successful and effective leadership can enhance levels of commitment, creativity and innovation. These leaders transform purpose into action.

Leadership is more than one person or position; it involves a complex moral relationship between individuals and groups.

Leadership is based on trust, obligation, commitment, emotion and a shared vision of the good.

Leaders can be a source of light for others, a light that illuminates that which both defines and obscures our true, authentic self.

Leaders can help their followers release their hidden potential, enabling them to see more clearly, recognise, discover, rediscover, seek and gaze more deeply.

Good leaders enable followers to excel beyond expectations by unifying their values and beliefs with higher levels of motivation, performance and morality.

Effective leaders augment the efforts, satisfaction and effectiveness of followers.

Leadership requires strong relationships. No one can be a leader without willing followers.

Developing Deeper Consciousness and Taking Compassionate Action

> *My brother's diminishing mental health was camouflaged by his hedonistic lifestyle. He had no awareness of his antagonistic, inflammatory behaviour. He would unleash rage, abusing strangers, friends and neighbours for no reason. He bullied those around him. He was blind to the impact he was having on others.*

Have you experienced an unhealthy relationship?

If you have been able to abandon this kind of relationship, describe how you were able to do this.

Were others aware of your situation before you realised this was happening?

If so, what blocked your awareness?

How can you protect yourself from being vulnerable to this happening again?

Were you aware of any mat carriers who helped and affirmed you? How did they love, support and guide you?

If you had a friend who was experiencing an abusive relationship, how could you guide and support them?

Reflect on the meaning of faith in your life.

How would you describe spiritual people?

What qualities stand out for people with a faith?

How do they compare to those who profess not to have a faith?

How would you describe heaven?

How would you describe hell?

Reflect on the nature of your lifestyle, such as where you live, your interests and pastimes?

Are there any changes you would like to make so that your life is more balanced and fulfilling?

What actions can you take towards achieving these changes?

Describe someone you know who has inspired you – personally or professionally.

How did this relationship affect your life?

How do you think you could inspire others?

> *Good people are vulnerable to suffering. Life is filled with pain, disillusionment and absurdity. God is no stranger to suffering, as seen in the crucified Jesus. But there is hope of new life in God.*

Chapter 14

Forgiving Dreams
(1996 – 1997)

Mary Anne felt drawn to move back to the north of England.

> *I felt a compelling mysterious call to travel back north to the land of my ancestors, nudged by a deep-seated, non-rational wisdom.*

At the same time a voice within was urging her to write to Andrew and say sorry for the hurt between them. He replied saying he had just been discharged from hospital after being sectioned and diagnosed with a paranoid personality disorder. He felt better knowing there was a name he could put to his behaviours. Mary Anne wrote to him again to tell him of her Christian faith and the way it had changed her life. Andrew replied that he too would welcome Jesus into his life.

Mary Anne accepted a new job and found lodgings with a member of the local church in a beautiful northern village. Both the job and her accommodation were not what she was expecting. Work was uninspiring, with poor leadership, while her landlady was vindictive, suddenly changing her contract so that Mary Anne could no longer stay at weekends.

Mary Anne started to spend more time with her parents and stayed with them for Christmas 1996. She spent many hours hiking across the countryside with her father. He seemed to be a changed man: calmer, gentle and humble, a far cry from the violent bully of the past. By grace, Mary Anne felt completely reconciled with him as he became the father he was intended to be. In contrast, her mother had not changed. If anything, her abusive traits had worsened. She was still attention-seeking and continually tried to goad and humiliate her husband.

Dad became acutely depressed and was admitted to a psychiatric ward for his own safety. Mum's constant taunts, combined with deep-seated memories of his difficult upbringing, were pulling him into a dark place.

The psychiatric ward was grim and the nursing staff seemed indifferent to the welfare of their patients. Although unwell, Dad was acutely aware of the poor behaviour of the staff. Many of the psychiatric patients were elderly widowers, who wandered round the ward lost and lonely.

Mary Anne read *God, Where Are You?* by Gerard Hughes, a book which gave her the resilience she needed to carry on. She gained strength and calm by surrendering herself to the situation she found herself in. She let go of her feelings of responsibility and accepted the chaos around her.

On one of her father's weekend visits home, Mary Anne discovered her mother was trying to poison him with paracetamol tablets crushed up in his tea. She was furious, but not surprised by her mother's wicked scheming. At a hospital review meeting her mother usurped the proceedings with her narcissistic and attention-seeking behaviour. This led to an argument in which the doctor sided with Mum, and Dad walked out in anger, returning home alone. Mum was admitted to the female psychiatric ward for overnight rest, after claiming she was exhausted by the strain of caring for her husband and at risk from his violent behaviour.

Intuitive Wisdom

> *I began to pray and listen. A voice within was guiding me to write to Andrew. I surrendered and began to write. I asked him to forgive me, as I forgave him. I was sorry for all the pain and hurt that had passed between us. I was sorry I hadn't been able to help him deal with his mental health problems. I felt at times I had not responded with the grace and patience he deserved.*

Life can feel mysteriously preordained instead of random and coincidental.

Seek forgiveness and take responsibility for the hurt you may have caused others.

Listen to the subtle language of God and a new light will illuminate your heart.

A personal journey of exploration into the mystery of God and human life can bring comfort and hope.

> *An unspoken language drifted between us, its message clear: reconciliation. This man had changed. His company felt tender-hearted and humble. The raging baboon from many years ago had metamorphosed into a gentle, quiet man. Other than the natural signs of ageing, his outward appearance was little different, but his inner transformation was profound. I felt a deep peace across my heartland. An inner beauty washed away and healed the wounds from the past.*

Without words or wishful request, reconciliation can visit your heart during long silences. This is the gift of grace.

This is a time for gentle silence, receptivity and awareness so as to listen to what is being said and not said.

There are things which can only be communicated within.

The grace of true pure acceptance can enable you to love in ways you never thought possible.

Weak leadership can create confusion and conflict within a team. Team members can feel insecure and bewildered. Performance will be affected and staff can experience harmful levels of stress.

> *She rapidly became the landlady from hell. Known to the church as the kindly widow of a local VIP, she was admired for her charity work, but behind this facade was a mean and nasty woman.*

Those who publicly masquerade as kind, benevolent and caring can be privately mean, nasty and cruel. A charitable facade can be a deliberate attempt to self-promote and gain popularity, a social platform for power and validation.

Following the death of a spouse, lives can be shattered and broken from the anguish of lost love.

It might be that an individual experiences more suffering on the inside of a psychiatric hospital than on the outside.

> *Even if patients weren't depressed before arrival, a stay of any length would certainly have rendered anyone, well or otherwise, mentally unfit. Many of them were elderly men admitted following the death of their spouses – lives shattered and broken from the anguish of lost love, wandering bereft souls unable to cope with life beyond the restraints of the psychiatric ward.*

Developing Deeper Consciousness and Taking Compassionate Action

> *Life can sometimes feel mysteriously preordained instead of random and coincidental.*

Reflect on this statement. Have you ever experienced this feeling?

Can you think of a time when you have forgiven yourself for your past actions or words?

What effect did this have on you?

How easy did you find this to do?

Can you recall a time when you have asked someone else for forgiveness for past hurts you may have caused?

Was the other person able to readily forgive you? If not, what do you think was blocking this?

What happened afterwards and how did this affect your relationship?

How can we as a society encourage one another to become more forgiving?

> *Within the dark building, its shadows fragranced by incense, I would fall to my knees in solitary prayer and weep, my body shaking with abject anticipatory grief: God, oh God, where are you? Please, please help me. Help my dad. Protect him from harm and surround him with loving, caring people.*

What does prayer mean to you?

Can you recall a time in your life when the power of prayer helped you find a way through a crisis?

If so, how did you pray and what happened as a consequence?

What would you say to a friend who is curious about how to pray?

> *I felt as if my God, my very own personal God, was closer to me than I was to myself. This gave me the resilience I needed to accept the chaos around and within me. I let go of trying to control these unfathomable circumstances. I let go of feeling responsible. I let the river carry me without struggling, trusting the water to take me to a place of unknown destiny.*

Can you recall a time in your life which felt chaotic?

As you look back, is this something you could have avoided?

What could be the gains as a consequence of the chaos?

Can you identify any mat carriers who helped and affirmed you?

Think of a time in your life when you felt content.

What do you believe enabled you to feel like this?

What can you do to repeat this so that you live a life which creates peace and contentment?

Chapter 15

Tormented to Death
(1997)

Mary Anne received a phone call from Lee: 'Dad has taken a massive overdose. The police had to break into the house to allow access for an ambulance crew. His heart stopped several times, but he is alive.'

As Mary Anne was driven to the hospital by her elderly neighbours she reflected on the inevitability of what was happening. From a young age she had known that Mum and Dad's dysfunctional relationship was going to lead to something like this.

> *I was frozen by anxiety as I strained to see through the sudden wall of darkness which surrounded my soul. I could neither pray nor cry. But I didn't doubt God's existence; the thought was too much to bear.*

The hospital consultant provided a bleak prognosis. Her father was on a life support machine and any further attempts to resuscitate him would be futile. It wasn't a question of *if* but *when* he would die. He had taken large quantities of pills and drunk Pernod, a potent liquor. This was his first and only attempt to take his own life.

All the family, Mum, Lee and Mary Anne, huddled around his bed. They said The Lord's Prayer and Psalm 51 with the hospital chaplain, then took turns to be alone with him to say their goodbyes. Mary Anne reminded Dad that she loved him.

At 4 a.m., as Mum was saying her farewells, Dad passed. She shrieked and Mary Anne and Lee rushed to the bedside to find her lying across her husband's deceased body.

Shocked and anguished, they drove home in the early morning silence. Mary Anne was frozen with dread. What would they find? She was relieved that the house felt peaceful with no signs of the trauma it had witnessed only a few hours earlier. But neither was there any note giving an explanation of Dad's actions. He had left nothing.

Mum looked like a ghost. She was broken. Meanwhile, Lee was raiding the bedroom drawers and cupboards searching for records of bank and saving accounts. 'Look how much Mum's worth!' he exclaimed. Mary Anne was disgusted by his insensitive and inappropriately gleeful behaviour.

Lee started to drink beer heavily and became agitated and aggressive. Mary Anne found some solitude on the back doorstep where she sat sobbing, clutching her knees to her chest like a child, desperate for consolation.

Mary Anne took charge of the funeral arrangements and was comforted by the Catholic priest who was to officiate the service. She was angered by the funeral director's sales pitch approach. When she called him out for his lack of respect he immediately changed his attitude.

She looked to her friend Julie for comfort and was bitterly disappointed to discover that Julie wanted nothing to do with her in her time of grief and sorrow. Instead, she left Mary Anne feeling shame and guilt at having shared her pain.

Intuitive Wisdom

> *I sensed the mystery of God in my deepest self. God was far beyond my thinking and imagination. I imagined being surrounded by God's holy angels who were helping to carry me through this terrible suffering. They would keep me company and soothe my wounded soul.*

Coping with a loved one's suicide is complex and traumatic.

> *There is something about the news of a suicide that cuts across everything we are doing or thinking. It has a chilling ring to it.*

Drugs and alcohol can be used in a futile attempt to drown the terror of grief and mourning. These will neither soothe, console nor alleviate the pain of loss. Only time and self-care, blended with the surrounding love and compassion of others, will carry us through.

> *Although we are never entirely immune from fear, anxiety and depression, if allowed to deepen, these negative emotions can separate and disconnect us from our true selves and our close relationships. We can become unreachable.*

When your heart becomes numbed by fear and suffering, death can seem the only escape from unendurable pain. You become unreachable by those who desperately try to save you.

In the crucible of death, each of us can graciously and passionately pay tribute as the life of our loved one closes. It is complete. As their inner light diminishes and silence deepens around us, we can thank them for who they are and remind them of our everlasting love.

✧

Those involved in providing funeral services can masquerade as kind and benevolent carers during a period of deep vulnerability. However, this can be a form of manipulation driven by financial profit.

> *When he'd finished talking I was so angry I wanted to shake him. I felt he had come to exploit our pain and sorrow. It was a profit-making exercise; he was a salesman selling fancy goods to the bereaved. He was implying that if we really loved Dad, then we'd be willing to have the best quality – and most expensive – wood, silk and accessories. The bereaved can ease their guilt by spending money; the more they spend, the greater their love and innocence.*

✧

> *I took her friendship for granted; I believed she could withstand watching and listening to my heart breaking. I was wrong.*

Although grieving is part of life, sharing inconsolable grief can permanently damage weak, fragile relationships. The power and impact of grief can overwhelm close friends and loved ones.

We can experience affirming strength and freedom during sacred conversations as they unlock an inner repository of unmet spiritual needs.

Unable to save our loved one from dying and death, we confront our own fallibility.

The hollowness and pain of sudden death can rob us of sweet nostalgic memories. We can feel as though everything has been taken from us, except the certainty and silence of death.

> *Dad left nothing behind other than dust and ash to scatter among the spring flowers and beauty of the earth.*

Developing Deeper Consciousness and Taking Compassionate Action

> *I have very few thoughts to recall. I was in shock as I travelled nearer and nearer to a situation which could only end tragically.*

Can you recall a time you received sudden and shocking bad news?

How did you cope? Were you able to surrender to the circumstances or did you resist and deny them?

Can you identify any mat carriers who helped and affirmed you? How did they love, support and guide you?

> *Bad things happen to good, holy people from loving families. No one is immune from suffering and tragedy.*

Sometimes life doesn't seem fair. How does this quote challenge your perception of suffering?

What do you consider to be of ultimate importance in life? How can you change your life to focus on these goals?

Chapter 16

Bare Dreams
(1997 – 1998)

The family try to come to terms with Dad's sudden death. Mum was a shadow of herself, utterly lost. Mary Anne was full of sadness, constantly looking back with thoughts of how things could have been different. She tried to cope by working harder as a way to manage the pain of Dad's death.

She soon noticed colleagues would avoid talking to her. She worried this was in case the conversation strayed into the uncomfortable reality of her father's suicide.

> *My grief and the stigma of suicide made others feel uncomfortable. Did it knock on their inner door of mortality, reminding them that they too would die?*

She felt shunned by most people, apart from one manager, Anna, who befriended her. Anna became a mat carrier. She invited Mary Anne to celebrate Christmas Day with her and her extended family. Mum had been invited to Lee's house but the invitation wasn't extended to his grieving sister.

A new director was appointed at Mary Anne's workplace. Young and ambitious, his overconfidence and miscalculations in a failing organisation resulted in a financial crisis which led to redundancies. Mary Anne was one of the casualties, but she also saw it as an excuse to get rid of the problem employee no one could face.

Her self-confidence and self-esteem were low. She felt like a vulnerable failure. After seventeen years of continuous public sector working she had to suffer the ignominy of visiting the unemployment office twice a week as a condition for her receipt of state support. The staff radiated mistrust. There was a sense that the unemployed were viewed as lazy. The atmosphere was grim and tense.

> *I would stand motionless in this grubby chaos, avoiding any facial expression or eye contact for fear of a scabby tattooed punch or blood-red Doc Marten shin kick. Losing my teeth would be the final straw!*

But this became an experience Mary Anne would learn to value. It reminded her of the hypocrisies of our so-called civilised society and gave her an opportunity to re-evaluate her own attitudes and prejudices towards the homeless and those living in poverty.

Despite her grief, Mary Anne needed to work. She would not allow this setback to disrupt her career, a career she loved. She had managed to crawl her way out of her difficult upbringing to create a life of independence, serenity and peace and she wasn't going to slide back now.

Intuitive Wisdom

> *Yet, in spite of this inner turmoil, just as in the days following Debbie's death in the nurses' residence in Cambridge, I was touched by the vivid beauty of life: strangers offering a quiet 'good morning', a faint smile from an innocent, shy child, and the bright yellow glow from endless fields of flowering rapeseed. The very act of living felt more precious, intense and glorious.*

Despite the pain and turmoil of grief, we can be blessed by a deeper appreciation of natural beauty, kindness and the joy of living.

During times of great suffering you can choose to ignore the betrayals of those who have harmed you. You can choose not to abandon them. To be anything other than loving, kind and patient would deny the existence of God and human vulnerability.

Following the death of a loved one by suicide, you can feel isolated by perceived stigma, self-blame and shame, experiencing feelings of betrayal and abandonment.

Inexplicable hope will reappear in your heart. This will calm, console and renew you. Remember, you are not what happens to you.

※

The unemployed and homeless are vulnerable people, anxious and afraid. For many, benefit sanctions threaten their ability to cope with serious hardship. It is fraught and grim; there is no light, no colour.

> *I felt both sadness and fear towards my kindred unemployed. Sad because many reminded me of Mum during the terrible years she suffered from alcoholism, tortured souls feeling worthless and dejected, powerless victims of desperate circumstances spinning out of control.*

Anyone can unexpectedly tumble into homelessness: redundancy, addiction, domestic abuse, bereavement, mental health problems, poverty. All can lead to having to live on the streets.

> *Being unwanted, unloved, uncared for, forgotten by everybody, I think that is much greater hunger, a much greater poverty than the person who has nothing to eat.*
> **Mother Teresa**

When faced with suffering, you can surrender your ego to grace and transform your pain into the energy of hope and optimism. You can accept the pain of being a human being.

We can transform our own pain and betrayals into simple acts of non-judgemental compassion and loving friendship.

> *This friendship generated a transformative power. I was surrounded by a beautiful circle of light, protecting, healing and strengthening me during these terrible days. It was a power which didn't take sides but offered a compassionate indifference to the events threatening my annihilation.*

The fresh sweetness of dawn always follows the darkness of night.

Whatever misfortunes befall us in life, we all share the same hopes and dreams, to love and be loved.

Developing Deeper Consciousness and Taking Compassionate Action

> *Our lives are defined by the moment the life of a loved one ends. Silence deepens as we begin our journey of grief.*

Recall a time in your life when you were grieving for a loved one.

How did you feel?

How did your grief affect your relationships?

What did you find helpful and comforting?

Can you identify any mat carriers who helped and affirmed you? How did they love, support and guide you?

What did you avoid or stop doing in order to cope?

How will this experience help prepare you for any further grief and loss?

> *When nothing else subsists from the past, after the people are dead, after the things are broken and scattered ... the smell and taste of things remain poised a long time, like souls ... bearing resiliently, on tiny and almost impalpable drops of their essence, the immense edifice of memory.*
>
> **Marcel Proust**
> Swann's Way

Were you aware of collateral beauty – a deeper beauty and meaning to life – as a consequence of your acute grief?

What can you share with others to help them cope with the loss of a loved one?

What are you more grateful for about your life, knowing that you will someday die?

How can you treasure and appreciate the people in your life more, knowing that they will someday die?

> *I have often described how kindness and compassion have transformed my life and enabled me to cope with suffering. This is what truly matters.*

> *My fortnightly visits to the dingy dole office with its barred windows and gritty light were humiliating and degrading. Outside, slumped and stumbling, were the local winos weeping and chanting to themselves, lost in a vapour of alcohol; I wondered if they were praying to be rescued from their enslavement to drink or from the world around them.*

In urban areas this is a familiar and heartbreaking occurrence. The young and old, male and female, regardless of race, ethnicity and class, can become enslaved by drugs and alcohol and find themselves begging for alms.

Have you ever overlooked the needs of the destitute and the homeless, including migrants and refugees?

Describe your attitude and feelings towards these people.

Identify what actions you can take to compassionately help the less fortunate.

How can you encourage others to join you in this?

Remember St Francis of Assisi's words: 'There but for the grace of God go I.'

Take some time to reflect on this and its meaning for you.

Reflection

The following reflection can help you move away from fear, doubt and anger, and move towards greater faith, hope, compassion and love. This is based on Ignatian Spirituality and the principles of consolation and desolation.

At the end of each day find a quiet place. Recall those moments which you have most enjoyed and list them. These do not have to be anything extraordinary. Instead, they can be everyday encounters, such as the beauty of a flower, the wonder of animals and wildlife, the laughter of a child or the gentleness of an elderly neighbour who greets you. Cherish these and give thanks to God. These moments are signs of God's self-giving presence and God's gifts to you.

Notice how these moments affected your mood during the day. This is how we move closer to God and become less self-absorbed and distracted. Our focus goes beyond ourselves and shows us where God is active in our lives. We feel a greater sense of joy and connection to our human community and the world of creation around us.

Now take some time to identify the moments you have least enjoyed and list them. Again these do not have to be anything extraordinary. They can be everyday experiences, such as doing your grocery shopping. Notice how these affected your mood. This time you may realise there were times you were impatient and frustrated. Consequently you were irritable and abrupt towards those around you.

This is how we move away from God as we become more self-obsessed.

This is where we are more concerned about ourselves and our ego and this separates us from our human community.

This drains us of our energy and vitality. We feel negative and pessimistic.

Chapter 17

The Prophecy is Realised
(1998 – 2000)

After five months of seeking a job of equal standing to the one she had left, Mary Anne was appointed clinical lead at a nearby private hospital. She was determined not to be demoted by her redundancy.

She was nervous about the culture in the private sector, which seemed to prioritise financial profit over genuine service to patients. The greed of the consultants with their facile charm repulsed her. Called to an operating theatre in the middle of a procedure, she was confronted by a child-like tantrum from the surgeon. Horrified by the lack of respect shown for the elderly naked unconscious patient on the operating table, Mary Anne made clear her refusal to accept this kind of behaviour.

Meanwhile, Lee and his wife Karen were scheming. They suddenly bought a large detached property, new cars, motorbikes and a large caravan. It was as though they had won the lottery. How could they afford such luxuries when neither of them was capable of earning more than the minimum wage? They seemed unusually keen for Mum to live with them.

Then Mary Anne met David in a chance meeting through a mutual acquaintance. He was seven years younger and they had very different outlooks on life. Although Mary Anne had neither the energy nor the inclination for romance, he was immediately attentive, showering her with gifts. She felt manipulated.

> *He seemed to be desperate to dive into a deep oceanic relationship, and his clinginess was dragging me down behind him.*

Mary Anne received the sad news that she sensed would come one day. It was inevitable. Andrew was dead. After drinking heavily, he had driven his car and crashed into a van. He died instantly. She declined the funeral invitation.

> *Andrew's sister invited me to his funeral. Fine threads of unresolved guilt at my inability to cope with his mental state meant I felt unworthy to attend. I was struggling to manage my grief after Dad's death and coping with a job that was threatening my integrity. I had little reserve to process the complexity of this sad news.*

Intuitive Wisdom

> *I felt infused with an unfamiliar gift of invisible grace, which was carrying me through this strange rocky landscape. Grace was my mat carrier.*

Trust in the mystery of grace to carry you through adversity.

~

When there are limited employment opportunities, with the risk of homelessness and destitution that accompanies a period of unemployment, accepting a job which postpones your true ambitions (deferred gratification) can protect your longer term aspirations.

~

> *I entered her office, closed the door and crept up to her. No words were spoken until I was a few inches away from her face. I was so close she could almost feel my breath. With piercing eyes and a calm voice, I raised a pointed finger to her face, and minaciously told her: 'Never ... never ... never ... subject my patients to such a degrading incident again.'*

Be valiant and challenge human indignity and degradation. When confronting the egos of the powerful, be prepared for retaliation in an attempt to discredit you. Choose your battles wisely.

Stay awake to the possibility of a hidden agenda that is not in your best interests. Be wise.

> *As the captain of my own ship, I was eager to ensure I remained on a seamless pilgrimage destined for horizons alive with beauty.*

Resist all those who try to dissuade you from pursuing your dreams. This could be more about their inner turmoil associated with fear, envy, resentment and self-interest, all of which are intended to subjugate and spoil your intentions.

Be true to your values so as to avoid exile from your true life script.

> *I was choking and feared he was engulfing me emotionally. I was drowning as I gasped for air, clutching the embankment with my fingertips.*
> *I was being slowly pulled in, despite my resistance.*

The grooming of adult females can be a subtle insidious process of manipulation and abuse. It can begin as friendship so that trust can be built up using gifts, charm and promises of happiness.

Unresolved guilt can interfere with decision-making, leading to regret and disappointment.

> *I offered a private requiem of prayers that his tormented soul was now at peace, free from suffering and brokenness.*

It is only though the darkness of death that a light appears. We can only come to know it through our lived experience of confusion, deep sadness and vulnerability.

Developing Deeper Consciousness and Taking Compassionate Action

> *Be valiant and challenge human indignity and degradation.*

Can you recall a situation when you challenged authority on behalf of someone in a position of vulnerability?

What skills did you need?

How did you feel before, during and after the event?

Would you do it again?

Can you recall a time when you overlooked an opportunity to stand up for the vulnerable?

What were the reasons for not intervening? How did you feel about this afterwards?

Do you choose to spend time with people who have similar values to you and take you closer to your true self?

How do you feel when you spend time with others who have conflicting values to yours?

Can you identify a situation when you have compromised your personal values?

Was this a conscious (aware) or unselfconscious (unaware) decision?

How would you advise and guide someone close to you who was struggling with a dilemma in which they are faced with a choice which could potentially compromise their values?

Chapter 18

A Secret Lie
(2000 – 2001)

Mary Anne was longing to find her soul mate and experience unconditional love, but without experience of that which she sought she was vulnerable to being misled. She was in danger of repeating old mistakes by choosing someone familiar who made her feel secure. David's persistent attention and gifts – perfume, jewellery, expensive meals and surprise weekends away – made her feel special at a time when she was emotionally fragile. Flattery drowned out feelings of guilt, grief and sadness. Moreover, it weakened her intuition.

Mary Anne's self-confidence took another blow as she started to suffer heavy menstrual bleeding and loss of bladder control. She was diagnosed with severe endometriosis affecting her ovaries, womb, bowel, bladder and pelvic cavity. She needed major surgery. The condition meant it was highly unlikely she would be able to have children. This news sent her thoughts into a spin. Combined with haunting childhood self-doubt, it caused her to feel a worthless failure. She now considered herself physically defective too.

David spoke about marriage, despite Mary Anne's diagnosis. She was troubled and confused, changed by the deaths of Dad and Andrew. David's apparent commitment was flattering and she was desperate to have a successful marriage.

> *The residue from my marriage to Andrew started to bubble and blister beneath the surface of my conscious self. I was painfully reminded of failure – highlighted by his recent tragic death – the guilt of not coping with his mental illness and of giving up so quickly on our marriage. Deluding myself with self-affirmation, I believed I could weaken these painful feelings by proving I was capable of a successful relationship.*

Intuitive Wisdom

> *I lied. I lied to my heart. I betrayed my own soul. I feebly gifted my trust to him and abandoned trusting myself. It was a deliberate naivety, which clung to denial and rejected the truth.*

In times of human vulnerability we can betray our soul in exchange for affection, affirmation and approval. Do not be afraid to disappoint others, despite how stressful and overwhelming it can feel.

You are not responsible for others' emotions. You have a responsibility towards others, but not for them.

※

> *At work I was self-conscious as I fretted about staining my clothes with pee or blood or both.*

Women with endometriosis can feel worthless, defective and unlovable.

The long-term effects of living with endometriosis can cause loneliness by adversely affecting social, professional and interpersonal relationships.

> *This chronic selective attention and outright denial of illness and pain was about to be shattered. Horrid, uncontrollable pain was forcing me into an unconditional surrender.*

Do not devalue the misery of pain and fear. It can only be abated by the truth. When suffering from a genuine physical illness, ask for help. Some things go beyond our ability to endure.

Ask yourself if your refusal to acknowledge pain, fatigue and stress is really a form of self-alienation, masquerading as concern over work and family pressures. Denying the truth will only exacerbate your suffering and prolong your healing.

※

When looking for answers to difficult questions, live with the prevailing silence. Do not rush, as silence itself can be the answer. Wait and allow time to wander to a place of empowerment, like a mountain stream which gathers volume and strength with distance.

Developing Deeper Consciousness and Taking Compassionate Action

> *My ego was being soothed and stroked. I allowed myself to venture into this mysterious land of illusion and fantasy. Like a defiant child in a cautionary tale, I disregarded my inner voice of wisdom whispering words of warning. Once again I succumbed to self-deception. I believed the lies I told myself. I was incapable of pulling back from the compulsion to prove my worth. I can do this. I can have a successful marriage.*

Describe your understanding of female adult grooming.

What can we do as a society to prevent this and help one another become more aware?

If you suspected someone was at risk what action would you take?

> *I lied. I lied to my heart. I betrayed my own soul. I feebly gifted my trust to David and abandoned trusting myself.*

Can you recall a time when you have ignored your inner voice?

What were the consequences?

What have you learned from this experience and what would you do differently if you sensed this happening again?

Who could support and guide you?

What can you do to help others who are experiencing something similar?

The silence of shame can engender regret for many years to come. The way back to the light of truth, authenticity and hope can be emotionally gruelling but essential for healing.

Think of a time when you or someone close to you felt shame. What effect did it have on you?

How can you overcome this?

How are you able to prevent this happening again?

Who can help and support you?

> *Which is the way forward? I felt as though time was running out as tomorrow became my today and today my yesterday. And still there were no clear answers. I had been altered by the pain of Dad and Andrew's deaths. Shame, blame and feelings of failure were blocking my senses.*

Describe how you resolve any past regrets.

How would you advise someone close to you who was struggling with shame and regret?

When looking for answers to difficult questions and decisions, how challenging do you find the prevailing silence?

What would you like to do differently when making difficult decisions or searching for answers to difficult questions?

Chapter 19

The Widowed Spinster
(2001 – 2003)

Mary Anne decided to marry David, despite her reservations about their compatibility. She would later discover that many of her friends had concerns about the marriage and disliked David but lacked the courage to say anything, reluctant to interfere.

They undertook weekly wedding preparation classes with the vicar. Mary Anne naively hoped this would ensure their marriage was embedded in Christian values. As the wedding day approached, she worried about how she would adjust to the loss of her single life.

> *I felt no excitement at the prospect of being together full time. I knew I would grieve for the silent beauty of living alone. In the depths of peaceful solitude I had found the gracious presence of God.*

Lee was the only family member to attend the wedding. Mary Anne, while upset, was not surprised that her mother, who was both mentally and physically fragile, could not (or would not) be there for her.

On the morning of the wedding Lee arrived at her flat and started drinking. He became belligerent and made defamatory comments about the sexuality of Mary Anne's male hairdresser who was helping her to prepare for her wedding. The atmosphere was tense and awkward. As Lee walked her down the aisle, Mary Anne wished her father was by her side.

> *My eyes filled with tears. Like the feet of ancient times, smiling through sorrow and carrying an invisible pain, we walked slowly down the aisle towards the white-robed vicar.*

Shortly after a chilly spring honeymoon, Mary Anne was admitted to hospital for major abdominal surgery. Her sole visitor the following day was a swaggering David boasting about his new toy, a recently purchased sports car. He brought no card, no flowers.

> *As I watched David from my bed, I realised the truth about our relationship. It was crystal clear. I wasn't being cherished by a loving, supportive husband – a grown-up. We were not in love with one another, but had been beguiled by the idea of love and marriage.*

Mary Anne was reminded that her childhood experiences had made her vulnerable to further grooming and abuse. David, far from romancing her, had actually been manipulating her.

> *This disastrous misjudgement was rooted in my childhood where I had learned to be brave, congenial and helpful when in fact I felt frightened, sad and angry. No one ever taught me how to learn from and embrace these emotions. As a consequence I could not rely on my internal warning system.*

Some months later Mary Anne felt unwell. She discovered that, at the age of 39, she was experiencing a premature menopause as a result of the surgery she had undergone. It was unlikely that she would conceive and if she did any pregnancy would probably end in miscarriage. The news on top of her diagnosis of endometriosis was devastating. She became consumed with an overwhelming desire to have a baby.

David's attitude towards Mary Anne suddenly changed. His charm faded and the gifts dried up. He intimidated her with long moody silences and began to display a cold, bitter tyranny. He constantly reminded Mary Anne of her shortcomings. Once again, her self-esteem was being harmed at the hands of others. She believed it was her fault and became subservient to him for fear of reprisals and ridicule.

One day David was sent home from work with mental health problems. He admitted he was suffering from depression and had been for some years. He had been looking for someone to empty his depression onto, and of course that person was Mary Anne. They paid for marriage and personal counselling. In addition to this David started to compulsively buy clothes, shoes and accessories as he concentrated on his fashion image. Mary Anne realised he was emotionally and psychologically shallow. In pursuing her he had been looking for a trophy wife to show off. An additional attraction was Mary Anne's higher income, which would help to fund his extravagant lifestyle.

Mary Anne turned again to her familiar way of coping and began to work harder. She gained a senior management position in the NHS. She also graduated with distinction in an MA in Leadership and Management. She felt an inner satisfaction that those cruel and disinterested schoolteachers, who had so easily written her off, were finally proved wrong.

Even though she had become a high-flying achiever and intellectually savvy at work, she was treated like an idiot at home.

Intuitive Wisdom

> *We discussed subjects such as commitment, finances, how we would deal with conflict, and our aspirations for the future. And still I ignored how we were made from different stuff. It was becoming more of a business transaction than a love story. At no point did either of us talk about being unsure.*

Although spiritual marriage preparation can help to embed your marriage in strong Christian values and deepen your readiness to live a married life, such classes bring no guarantee of happiness. You may still be tested in ways you did not anticipate. Some things remain hidden and may take considerable time to manifest themselves.

> *They hoped it would be happily ever after, but feared our marriage was doomed to fail and that it would only be a matter of time. Their dark worries lay in hibernation like dormice curled up asleep in their nest next to hazelnuts. The long winter of my soul was encased in a silent frozen climate.*

If you sense a friend is ignoring warning signs of potential relationship problems which could involve domestic abuse, find the courage and integrity to share your concern. Your observations and intuition could help to prevent future pain and suffering.

Before making a lifelong commitment, ask yourself if you are truly in love with one another, or simply beguiled by the idea of love and marriage.

Having the courage to undo a decision, to disregard what you once believed would make you happy, may avoid robbing you of your essential integrity, which is a pearl of great price.

※

At some stage in our lives we all smile through sorrow and carry an invisible pain.

Constant negativity transmitted onto you can be internalised. Eventually you become a slave to these opinions. You lose your individuality and true identity as you become defined by another's contempt for you.

Fear of failure can create false commitment and long-term suffering.

Be alert to gaslighting – controlling behaviour that can result in you believing things about yourself that are not true. For example, that you are over-reacting to situations or that your memory is unreliable.

Turn away from hopelessness and find what makes your heart sing, such as glimmers of beauty in the natural world, human kindness and the sweetness of friendship.

Developing Deeper Consciousness and Taking Compassionate Action

'The widowed spinster' is a deliberate contradictory term I created to explain the Church's response to my request for a church wedding following my divorce from Andrew. Despite this divorce occurring before I became a Christian, my request was initially denied. However, when the minister realised Andrew was deceased this decision was immediately reversed. I was now considered a widow instead of a divorcee, which allowed the church to grant me a Christian wedding.

What are your assumptions about a couple seeking a church wedding?

What are your thoughts about my response to how the Church viewed me, which generated the term 'widowed spinster'?

What are your views about divorced people remarrying in church?

⁓

Fear of failure and of disappointing others is demoralising and can precipitate perilous decisions.

Can you recall a time when you regretted making a decision which was taken against a background of fear of failure or fear of disappointing someone?

What would you like to do differently next time?

What are the challenges you would face?

How can you overcome these and your fear of failure?

Who can support and guide you?

How can you let go of past regrets?

⁓

Describe your understanding of the term 'gaslighting'.

Have you experienced gaslighting?

How did it affect you and what action did you take?

What can you do to prevent this happening again? Are there any barriers which could challenge your ability to prevent this reoccurrence?

If you knew someone who was at risk of this what would you do to support and guide them?

> *I experienced a moment of sudden enlightenment. As I watched David from my bed, I realised the truth about our relationship. It was crystal clear. I wasn't being cherished by a loving, supportive husband – a grown-up. We were not in love with one another, but had been beguiled by the idea of love and marriage.*

Can you recall a moment of sudden enlightenment?

Reflect on a time when your intuitive understanding of a person close to you deepened and you gained fresh insights into his or her character. Describe this experience and how it happened. How did it affect your thoughts, feelings and behaviour – for better or worse – towards this person?

> *Turn away from hopelessness and find what makes your heart sing, such as glimmers of beauty in the natural world, serving others, human kindness and the sweetness of friendship.*

As I became alienated by life at home, I turned away from hopelessness and threw myself into my work and MA studies.

What makes your heart sing and enables you to turn away from hopelessness?

How do you ensure this joy is part of your everyday life?

During times of hopelessness, can you identify any mat carriers who have helped and affirmed you? How did they love, support and guide you?

If you noticed someone close to you was experiencing hopelessness what could you do to support and affirm them?

Chapter 20

Sophia
(2003 – 2004)

Mary Anne felt suffocated by their busy urban lifestyle with its emphasis on the ego-serving trappings of materialism. They moved to a small village in the countryside.

> *I had arrived. I had been called to a place where I could breathe again. Exhausted by the demands of work and the strain of coping with David's controlling dependency, my soul had been gracefully guided to a secret, undiscovered sanctuary.*

David continued to make her life difficult. She was concerned that they were socially isolated. Her friends were discouraged from visiting and when they did David threw a tantrum once they had left. His emotional absence and constant bullying echoed her father's behaviour.

There was another lurid similarity between Dad and David: just as Dad had frequented strip clubs, Mary Anne discovered David was addicted to internet pornography.

> *David's blatant lies and ugly lusting after other women's bodies made me feel sick. He was vulgar and warped.*

Mary Anne was livid but at the same time wondered if she was to blame. Did David find her unattractive? There was little physical intimacy between them. She tried to help him, the memories of Andrew's addiction and mental health issues still fresh in her mind. There was more counselling, including with the local priest.

In her desolation, Mary Anne concentrated on her garden, seeking solace in nature. She tried to protect herself, her self-esteem, even her sanity, by doing the things she loved and believed in.

A two-day spiritual retreat in which Mary Anne learned about the concept of spiritual companionship proved to be a life-changing moment. The chaplain at the hospital she was working in introduced her to Clare who would become her close spiritual companion over the next seven years.

> *Clare was my mat carrier. Through our loving friendship I developed a profound connection with God. My life filled with reverence, beauty, wonder and awe as Clare graciously helped me navigate through life's wayward storms.*

Then Mary Anne discovered she was pregnant. Her dearest wish had been granted, she was to be a mother. She was filled with joy.

> *My prayers had been answered! I was pregnant. I was going to be a mum. I would be able to put right all the wrongs that had happened to me during my blighted childhood.*

Although Mary Anne was elated, David was shocked and bewildered.

Mary Anne imagined her unborn baby to be a daughter. She called her Sophia, which means wisdom.

A few days before her first antenatal scan the wonderful dream of having a child was shattered as Mary Anne woke early one morning with severe pelvic pain and bleeding. She was rushed to hospital in an ambulance. The baby had died. As she lay in her hospital bed she asked to see the chaplain, but he was too busy to visit her, in spite of her repeated requests. She felt abandoned by God and the Church. During the weeks that followed Mary Anne was appalled at how miscarriages can be trivialised by society. She felt isolated and unloved.

Meanwhile, she was concerned to discover that her mother was moving three hundred miles away from her hometown to live on the south coast with Lee and Karen. Surely this would not end well. Her mother had always been threatened by Karen's youth and jealous of her marriage to Lee. Lee was the husband Mum had never had and their relationship was uncomfortably close.

> *They were entangled in some kind of oedipal symbiosis. They could neither live with nor live*

> *without each other. It reminded me of Mrs Morel and her son Paul from Sons and Lovers, it was unhealthy and obsessive.*

Intuitive Wisdom

> *Like a moth flying into a flame, he was drawn to horrid adulterous images; nothing else could satisfy him, they owned his eyes and his heart. He was willing to risk our marriage so that he could dance once more to the haunted music with his fatal beloved pornography.*

An addiction to pornography can obstruct physical and emotional intimacy, leading to a breakdown of trust in a relationship. Its impact can be compared to adultery. It is a betrayal that can traumatise the partner as the relationship disintegrates. Thus, what is meant to be a sacred and loving relationship becomes one fraught with anguish, pain and disillusionment.

Only by confronting relational problems will you begin to find freedom, healing and hope. Set yourself free from the chains you revere before your senses are dulled and you become helpless and powerless.

༺༻

> *I needed to recover my voice and find freedom from silence, oppression, shame, blame and marginalisation by disclosing the truth.*

The cultural ego-serving trappings of greed, consumerism and adoration of celebrities can lead to insecurity and dissatisfaction with your life. Your soul needs to breathe and be stripped of illusions and pretence. A simple unmaterialistic lifestyle is more likely to bring lasting happiness and peace.

Do not be a slave to money. Live within your means and avoid debt. Financial stability can bring peace and happiness.

Avoid consuming more than you need.

❦

Natural earthy country smells and wild beauty can lift your senses as they guide you to the threshold of your soul. The calls of migrating geese can carry your imagination to enchanted places and a living encounter with God's grace.

❦

Without experiencing brokenness you cannot change and without change you cannot grow and thrive. This is the window to God.

❦

Find your soul friend, someone who will never deceive and flatter you and will always walk with you, defend you and selflessly love you. They will teach, guide and listen with their heart; they will offer wisdom and compassion. Ultimately their wish is for you to find true happiness.

Life-changing decisions are not to be taken hastily, especially when you are lonely, vulnerable and sick. Seek the wisdom of others to guide and protect you.

Like a prudent archaeologist, with the help of your soul friend you can sift through layers of history and recover and analyse stories and images from your inner landscape. This will expand your awareness of life in God, as wisdom and spiritual insights dawn within your consciousness. These spiritual musings can enable you to grow and develop; it is a cherished intimate journey with God.

❦

Becoming pregnant is a small miracle being nursed inside a warm and loving womb.

A mother's rich dark red womb is an inner sanctuary and a home for the unborn child. Eventually, there is birth as light approaches from an unlived world.

Miscarriage at any stage of pregnancy can be extremely distressing; the unlived dream bears no proportion to the duration of the pregnancy. It is a misunderstanding that a woman will experience less grief if she loses the baby early on.

After the loss of a baby it is not unusual for the mother to feel a sense of guilt, even though she may know that the loss could not have been prevented. Self-blame and a deep attachment to the child can have a devastating impact on the mother, and the father too, which can be experienced for many years. This invisible loss is profound. All too often it is a taboo subject in society.

Grief can feel like an impervious place of nothing and nowhere, a dark void within and outside.

Developing Deeper Consciousness and Taking Compassionate Action

Do you agree that addiction to pornography is physically and emotionally harmful?

What can we do as a society to minimise exposure to pornography for vulnerable people, especially for children and young adults?

༺༻

How can you resist the prevailing culture of greed, consumerism and shallow adoration of celebrities?

༺༻

In this chapter I develop a long-term relationship with a spiritual companion, also known as my soul friend.

How does a soul friend differ from someone who is a good friend?

What would you like to gain from a soul friend?

༺༻

Can you describe the moment you first discovered you – or your partner or friend – were pregnant.

What were your thoughts and feelings?

How did it change your outlook on life?

Were there any surprises about how you responded to this pregnancy?

> *This invisible loss is profound and, all too often, a taboo subject in society.*

What are your thoughts about this statement?

What can we do as a society to help those who are grieving through miscarriage?

How would you help to console someone who has experienced a miscarriage?

Chapter 21

An Invisible Loss
(2004 – 2008)

It was Christmas 2004 and Mary Anne was feeling desolate, numb with grief. Everywhere were reminders of the child she had lost, from the baby Jesus to happy families celebrating the festival together.

She planted a tree to commemorate her unborn child, Sophia. Apart from the memories of what might have been, this was the only testament to the short life of her unborn baby. There was no funeral service or grave to visit.

Given her failing marriage to David, Mary Anne decided to remain childless; she could not tolerate him being the father of her child. Of course she realised that in any case conception would be extremely unlikely given her medical history of endometriosis, but her decision made her feel as if she had some control over her life.

> *I chose to remain childless. This was one of the toughest decisions I have ever made. It was as though the yearning stranger in me was telling me: 'This is for your sake'. There was a secret path before me where hidden treasures were yet to be revealed. I felt as though I was being guided by a prophetic whisper and I had a deep knowing that I was being taken care of.*

Mary Anne applied for an innovative new role at a northern university. The new job gave her purpose again and she thrived on the boundless enthusiasm of the students.

She adopted a puppy retriever called Bethany. She needed another creature to take care of and nurture:

> *The darkness of not loving frightened me. I feared that if I did not love then I wouldn't exist.*

Her healing love for Bethany saved Mary Anne.

> *My feelings of worthlessness and emptiness were being transformed into a healing love. I was no longer emotionally bankrupt and craving affection, but was bursting with excitement and deep gratitude to the divine. I was trusting God more than ever.*

She started to have horse riding lessons and quickly discovered she had a powerful emotional connection with these majestic creatures. Both her new canine and equestrian friends were showing her trust, forgiveness and unconditional love. She felt more connected to her inner self:

> *I felt connected to this stranger in me, who is more ancient and mysterious and more in tune with the rhythms of nature and her seasons. I was in harmony with myself and the natural world.*

Mary Anne was increasingly worried about her mother. After a pitiful phone call from her, she became concerned about her health and wellbeing so she took leave from work and headed south to visit. Mum was in a shocking state of malnourishment and neglect, uncared for by Lee and Karen. The only time Lee saw her was to demand money. He was now controlling her finances.

Mary Anne arranged for Mum to be admitted to a nursing home for respite care. A couple of weeks later she returned to live with Lee and Karen but soon afterwards was admitted to hospital after a domestic fight. Mum never left hospital again. She was diagnosed with cancer and died penniless, her bank accounts wiped clean to fund the hedonistic lifestyle of her son and daughter-in-law. At the funeral Lee and Karen offered not a single word of tribute towards the eulogy.

After she returned home, Mary Anne wrote to them about their appalling treatment of Mum and asked them never to contact her again.

> *But my saddest memory of Mum is that, despite my hope and longing, she never said she was sorry for all the hurt and pain she caused me. I never once*

heard her express regret for the poisonous regime she had subjected me to as I was growing up. But while she may have stunted my vitality as a child living in constant fear of punishment, she never succeeded in obliterating my authentic expression of my true self.

It was clear to Mary Anne that Lee was a distillation of all the worst traits of their parents, an angry and emotionally cold bully as well as a devious self-serving individual who was not to be trusted. He could have taken a different path in life but chose not to.

Intuitive Wisdom

No tinsel, baubles and twinkling fairy lights were used to decorate our home. The house was devoid of any outward signs of joy. Christmas was all about babies, mums, dads, brothers and sisters. All around were nativity plays, small children carrying their Christingle oranges, and carols depicting wonderful scenes of the birth in the stable.

Involuntary childlessness is a lonely and barren place to live in. The loss of the dream of a family can be devastating.

Despite the pain and grief you may be experiencing, trust there is a deeper and higher purpose to your life not yet revealed.

Our pets can embody unconditional love and divine beauty. Dark shadows of suffering can disappear in the radiant joyful light of our pets' playfulness and loving companionship.

Pets can become our soul's healers and restorers as we learn to trust them without feeling vulnerable. It is through their humble love we can trust, hope and dream.

Fresh natural beauty and magic can be encountered as we explore new wild places in the company of our pets.

By spending quiet time with horses you will discover an emotional connection and rhythm which brings clarity, hope, peace and contentment deep within your soul.

There is a kind of ancestral echo within the soul which is sensitive to these majestic beings. They can teach you collaboration and humility, never domination. This evokes a deeper sense of gratitude, affection, privilege and humility as they awaken a more compassionate, patient and loving spirit within you. You are in harmony with yourself and the natural world. This is a blessed state of equanimity.

> *I was hopelessly in love. Something shifted in me as I experienced a deep synchronicity with these amazing, graceful creatures. I discovered an emotional connection and rhythm with them and with the natural world around me. A mysterious spirit was ensuring I was made aware of the life and love of horses. It was as though I had been asked what I knew of God, and I silently blossomed like a cherry tree.*

Developing Deeper Consciousness and Taking Compassionate Action

> *Christmas 2004 was empty. Surrounded by images of children, from baby Jesus to the quintessential family sharing Christmas together, I withdrew deep into my inner recluse sending no cards and giving no gifts. There was a darkness deep inside me which matched the dark winter outside.*

After my miscarriage shortly before Christmas 2004 I was empty. I felt barren and hollow with intense emotional pain and mental misery. I was on the road to nowhere as I mourned my invisible loss. I daydreamed about my lost pregnancy.

Can you recall a time when you experienced a significant loss? For me it was my pregnancy and the dream of becoming a mother.

What were the difficulties when facing your loss?

How did you deal with this?

Were there any surprises or unintended consequences?

Did you make any changes as a result of this loss? If so, describe how these influenced your life. What were you hoping to gain by these?

How has this affected who you are today?

As you reflect, can you identify any mat carriers who helped and affirmed you? How did they love, support and guide you?

※

> *Pets can become our soul's healer and restorer as we learn to trust them without feeling vulnerable. It is through their humble love we can trust, hope and dream.*

Do you have any examples of the healing power of pets?

> *Fresh natural beauty and magic can be encountered as we explore new wild places in the company of our pets.*

Reflect on this statement. Have you ever had a similar experience? If so, how would you describe it to a friend?

> *By spending quiet time with horses you will discover an emotional connection and rhythm which brings peace and contentment deep within your soul. And so, when asked what you know of God your soul will silently blossom like a cherry tree.*

Can you think of a pet or other animal which brings contentment deep within your soul?

Do you agree that animals and pets can be our mat carriers, carrying us to places of clarity, hope, beauty, healing and peace by their love and companionship?

Chapter 22

Herons and Horses
(2008 – 2011)

After her mother's death Mary Anne found herself in a spiral of despair involving her work, marriage and health.

David was increasingly hostile. He craved material possessions: expensive clothes, better cars and exotic holidays, but he was never satisfied; it was never enough. He was angry and resentful that Mary Anne didn't inherit any money from her mother and frustrated that he had been passed over for promotion at work. He wasn't realistic about money, his abilities or career prospects.

Mary Anne felt burdened by guilt about the deaths of Andrew, Dad and Mum.

> *There was always more I could have done: loved more, cared more, helped more, forgiven more. Guilt and shame paralysed me.*

Work was becoming intolerable, the atmosphere toxic. Those at the top of the organisation had been promoted beyond their level of competence, achieving their success by treading others underfoot. Everything was ruled by money, with students herded onto programmes for commercial benefit. Covert bullying was an accepted part of the culture. Mary Anne played no part in this, but instead concentrated on her primary focus: to help the students realise their true potential. She often drove home from work in tears.

During this turmoil she was given a precious gift by a stranger: a strong loving bond with a horse called Charlie. In all weathers he whisked her away from her troubles, across meadows and clear streams, across snow-covered fields and through autumn mists.

> *The sound of the flowing water cleansed my soul, carrying away the dust and grit of worry. Beneath*

> *the shadow of the hunchback prehistoric blue-grey heron and dancing acrobatic swallows, shy deer accompanied us on our way home.*

Mary Anne admitted to her GP, Dr Wong, that she had increasing issues with her bladder, bowel and womb. She endured invasive procedures to investigate the cause and eventually was told she had to undergo more surgery. She tried to find out more about what would be involved and the risks of the operation, but the doctor seemed to find her questions trivial and irritating. He was more excited about the hospital's new colorectal surgeon who would be performing her surgery than addressing her concerns.

When she met her surgeon he seemed distracted and uninformed about Mary Anne's medical history. Reluctantly she agreed to the surgery.

Intuitive Wisdom

> *Faced with inescapable suffering, some choose to live an inward life inside their own heart, companioned by their sheltering soul. It's like an interior monastery where they are the only human inhabitants. They have built a sanctuary of resistance where no one else can visit.*

When faced with perpetual unhappiness some find solace by living an inward life.

Jealousy of those who are perceived as having suffered less hardship can lead to resentment. This can be hurtful and destructive to relationships, leading to isolation and the burden of regret and guilt.

For some, endurance of pain and hardship can be a self-inflicted penance, a form of punishment and self-blame in an attempt to compensate for past failed relationships.

The spirit of the horse is authentic, respectful, trusting, empathetic and forgiving. This rapport can touch your soul in

unprecedented passionate and inspiring ways. Despite their majestic size and strength, they are served by gentleness, patience and grace. Capable of such power and yet not violent.
So beautiful, without vanity.

By sharing the rarefied reality of the horse you can experience unconditional intimacy and a deep synchronicity which your soul longs for.

> *There is a deep peace in those precious paradise moments, where no thought, no act and no words can disturb the beauty of the friendship of the horse. You feel wild and awake in their presence as you discover your true equanimity.*

Be alert to the culture of an organisation. Ask yourself who is admired, rewarded and promoted. Is it those who engender toughness, competitiveness and insensitivity, or is those who foster collaboration, fairness and equality?

> *The most lucrative, prestigious jobs tend to cause the greatest harm. The most useful workers tend to be paid the least and treated the worst. If you possess one indispensable skill – battering and blustering (like a rugby player) your way to the top – incompetence in other areas is no impediment. The wrong traits were rewarded, as those who rose to the top were conformists and sycophants.*
>
> **George Monbiot**
> How Did We Get Into This Mess?

Pay attention to leaders who…
- Spend more time talking than listening. Tune into the specific details of their narrative and avoid becoming bemused by their chatter.
- Seem over-confident. Instead look for competence, compatibility and capability.
- Seem perpetually busy and distracted. Look for good work achievements and action-orientated outcomes.

When faced with organisational change it may be wise to carry on with a quiet conviction and an unequivocal intrinsic purpose.

Be wary of a readiness to unquestionably accept medical explanations to alleviate the anxiety of uncertainty and not knowing.

> *Despite knowing I was more certain about my questions than I was about the faint answers I was getting, after a few months of deliberation I decided to go ahead. I was living with ongoing suspense and anxiety.*

The unconditional kindness of a stranger is a priceless gift and sacred blessing.

Developing Deeper Consciousness and Taking Compassionate Action

> *In quiet conversation awaken friendship and intimacy as you each gently offer the gifts of love and light.*

Can you recall a time when you have experienced such a rapport with an animal companion or perhaps a friend or partner?

If this is something you would like to experience, how could you make it happen?

> *I had a mounting sense of incompatibility with this toxic, bullying culture. I began to feel drained and started to distance myself from the system to avoid becoming infected. Violations of trust and integrity caused me to withdraw. The creeping imposition of autocratic power was eroding any sense of democracy. There was a pessimistic assumption that staff and students were to be mistrusted as they were fundamentally lazy.*

What are the challenges of working in a team?

What are the benefits of working in a team?

Describe how you would motivate and lead a team.

Describe your experience of organisational culture, both good and bad.

※

> *[The surgeon] was disengaged and distracted and made me feel as though I was wasting his time: he was too busy and too important for my trivial case. My quest for information was an irritation. I wanted him to realise that I was frightened and that I needed to understand the risks and benefits of the operation. I wanted him to assuage my fears. I knew it was serious and complicated.*

Despite knowing I was more certain about my questions than I was about the faint answers I was getting, after a few months of deliberation I decided to go ahead.

With patient wisdom place more certainty in your questions rather than being eager to accept the substance of the answers in an endeavour to allay the worry of uncertainty.

Reflect on this statement.

If you have been in a similar situation, how easy did you find the decision-making process? Were you able to take your time or did you feel compelled to make an instant decision?

What happens if you approach a problem/decision from a stance that is the opposite to the one you normally prefer?

How would this influence you if something similar happened to you now?

※

> *The unconditional kindness of a stranger is a priceless gift and sacred blessing.*

Can you describe a time when you were given such a gift?

How did it influence your outlook on life?

How did you express your gratitude?

How easy do you find it to accept a gift from others?

If you find it difficult, how can you change how you feel so that you can easily accept gifts?

How do you feel when you have given a gift to someone?

Chapter 23

A Sanctimonious Halo
(2011 – 2013)

In April 2011 Mary Anne underwent abdominal mesh surgery to repair a torn wall in her bowel. She was given no medical explanation as to what had caused this, despite her requests. Nor was she offered an alternative option.

Fourteen months later, feeling very unwell, she visited her GP. Dr Wong seemed sceptical of Mary Anne's description: 'It's like an alien monster and my body wants rid of it!' She felt as if she was rotting from the inside. Despite her complaints, hospital doctors and consultants were also sceptical that Mary Anne's symptoms could be attributed to the mesh. Her protestations went unheard for many months, which led to further deterioration in her health and wellbeing.

Far from being supportive and caring, David seemed disgusted by Mary Anne's symptoms:

> *His resentment towards me grew stronger day by day as his trophy wife was no longer available for display.*

Mary Anne continued to work when she should have taken sick leave. As she outwardly appeared to be well, she feared she wouldn't be believed but labelled as suffering from stress and not coping with her work. Disabled toilets were emergency sanctuaries as her unpredictable bowel became uncontrollable.

In February 2013, her symptoms worsening, Mary Anne visited Dr Wong and was signed off work. Cold and weak, she only left her bed for short walks to visit the bathroom. She was thankful for the company of her black and white cat, Chuckles, who brought warmth and comfort as she slept tucked up to Mary Anne.

Mary Anne was puzzled by subtle changes in David's behaviour.

He seemed uncharacteristically happy. One night she checked his phone to discover he was having an affair with one of her friends at the stables.

> *Their clandestine affair described through the texts was vulgar and repulsive. When I look back now, it seems inevitable but at the time the obvious had become unrecognisable until pain and chaos stripped away my self-made denials.*

She asked David to leave. Even through her illness and pain she felt relieved.

> *But in my brokenness I felt a purification as my self-awareness finally emerged. I had spent years pretending I was happy with David. I had betrayed myself by ignoring my true feelings so I could accommodate his. I had abandoned my true self. David packed a bag and left. He should have gone a long time ago.*

With the help of her friends Anna and Beverly, Mary Anne began to sort out her affairs. Her priority was to separate her finances from David as he was spending lavish amounts from their joint account on his new girlfriend. She appointed a lawyer to deal with divorce proceedings.

In July 2013, still facing scepticism from the medical profession that her increasing ill health was due to the mesh implant, Mary Anne was admitted to hospital for a hysterectomy.

Intuitive Wisdom

> *When you agree to undergo surgery you will submit your body and soul to volatile gases and colourful injectable anaesthetic agents. It is like a pond swallowing a stone as you sink into oblivion.*

Undergoing any invasive medical procedure can feel degrading and humiliating as well as frightening. It requires courage and trust on your part, and empathy and compassion from those responsible for undertaking the procedure.

༺ ༻

A draconian performance management approach with the implicit threat of constructive dismissal can force staff to work when unwell. The threat of power and policy used to punish staff and protect the employer can be intimidating and oppressive.

༺ ༻

Do not assume the absence of a visible disability means that one doesn't exist.

༺ ༻

During intense suffering, time becomes blurred. Days and nights are blended into one. This distance from reality can bring enlightenment.

> *Chained to my vows I had tolerated abuse for years. His final betrayal granted me permission to protect myself and evict his creepy, sordid presence. Before he went, his last words to me were that he was fed up with my sickness and our loveless marriage. He knew he was behaving badly but believed that the wrongdoing was necessary to bring things to a head.*
> *There was no gentleness and no love between us. Any sense of affection had gone sour.*

A person with narcissistic characteristics may enact these with passive-aggressive behaviours. These can present as blaming and scapegoating their partner. Instead of owning their responsibilities, they choose to adopt the 'poor me' role, convincing themselves they have a licence to break the bond of trust with their partner.

The dread of change and the inevitable losses associated with a broken marriage can lead to an inability to end the relationship. The idea of losing your security, being abandoned and rejected, can be terrifying.

When we are troubled and sick, our pets can provide companionship. Our pain and vulnerability can make us feel unlovable, but our pets can tell us otherwise. Their presence can feel divine as our craving for attachment is met. Our pets may just be fulfilling their destiny by being by our side.

Simple acts of human and animal kindness with soft words and tenderness can carry us to places of restoration and healing.

> *I was also afraid of the power of the medical profession. I needed them to provide information for my employer to enable me to continue to receive an income while I was sick.*

Medical abandonment and alienation can threaten a patient's mental health, trust and security.

Fear of harm and wrongful judgement can silence and trap you into believing you are powerless.

Developing Deeper Consciousness and Taking Compassionate Action

> *Please do not assume the absence of a visible disability means that one doesn't exist.*

Do you think this assumption is prevalent in today's society?

Would you intervene if you witnessed an individual being discriminated against because their disability was not observable? For example, use of a dedicated parking space or access to toilet facilities.

Have you ever experienced making a complaint about receiving an inadequate or poor standard of public service, either for yourself or on behalf of another?

How did this affect you and those you were representing?

What was your response? Did you succeed in being listened to?

What would you do differently next time?

How has this influenced your perception of healthcare, education or social care?

Can you recall a time when you have felt betrayed by someone close to you?

What effect did this have on you and your relationship with them?

Were you able to discuss this with them so they were aware of your feelings? If not, why not?

> *In the face of betrayal, by confronting the truth, the veil of deceit can been lifted, the smog can disappear. You will see more clearly. Like the return of a graceful migrating bird your serenity will emerge. The oppression will evaporate, as the truth within your soul is unleashed.*

Chapter 24

Surviving the Stitch-up and Smiling Through Pain
(2013 – 2014)

This was one of the darkest and most difficult periods in Mary Anne's life. Her hysterectomy had to be aborted on the operating table. The effects of the surgical mesh implant meant that her pelvic anatomy was distorted and any attempt to surgically remove her womb would be dangerous and life threatening.

It was during this period that Mary Anne realised who her true friends were: those who offered her unconditional support, both practical and emotional. Those friendships that only offered opinionated judgement she left to dwindle and wither away. Despite the fear of loneliness, she decisively abandoned them.

Wendy, a neighbour who had heard of Mary Anne's plight, offered to help in any way she could. She would be there whenever Mary Anne needed her. This unconditional compassion and support changed Mary Anne's preconceptions of friendship and confirmed her decision to turn her back on those old friends who were so quick to judge.

She was getting sicker day by day, until one night she believed she was dying. A call to her GP went unanswered and so she asked a friend to drive her to the hospital where she begged for help. After an emergency CT scan, her consultant, agitated and nervous, told her she needed urgent surgery. Her bowel was perforated and she was septic.

> *I went to theatre weak and empty, wondering if I would ever wake up. I had neither the energy nor motivation to care, just a few lingering thoughts that my animals would need to be looked after.*

She awoke from surgery to discover she had undergone a colostomy. The surgeon had intended to remove the mesh but Mary Anne was too sick and the procedure too dangerous. He warned her that she would need further life-changing surgery.

> *Not only had my inner anatomy been ravaged by endometriosis and the nylon mesh, but my outer appearance was affected too, like a carefully crafted sculpture which had been defaced by ugly and angry graffiti.*

She remained in hospital for two weeks with sweet thoughts of her animals comforting her through the pain of recovery. She returned home with a stoma.

> *As I entered the house I could feel the stoma bag moving across my tummy, a slippery warm foreign body sliding randomly across my skin. I went upstairs to the bathroom. The bag had become dislodged and I had poo all over my abdomen and clothes.*

As she tried to adapt to her new reality she had dark thoughts of unemployment, debt and homelessness, all the things she had tried so hard over the years to avoid by working hard and learning new skills. Her self-esteem was low and her femininity crushed by the foreign body attached to her abdomen.

But then Mary Anne's fearless inner teenager returned, giving her the determination to start rebuilding her life. Her first priority was to find somewhere to live, somewhere tranquil. She rejected advice to rent a property, unwilling to repeat the experience of the exploitative landlords she had encountered in the past. Instead, she bought a cottage in a small village. She immediately loved the house and the beauty of the rural setting. Nostalgic images of Nanna and Grandad's house stirred feelings of peace and security.

> *I made new friends, which helped to minimise social isolation. These were shy, authentic folk unaffected by greed and externality. They had a natural kindness, which did not attract attention to itself. Nor did they take advantage of my*

> vulnerability. They lived quietly and observantly; they too had known hard times. Each offered support when things were difficult and were ready to celebrate happy, joyous occasions. They were considerate and gentle both in their words and actions.

Her recovery was difficult but made bearable because of the unconditional loyalty and friendship of her animals and close circle of friends. However, money was tight. She was forced to claim insufficient state benefits and resorted to selling her jewellery, furniture and clothes to cover the bills until she was well enough to return to work, if she would ever be able to work again.

Surgeons disagreed about the next course of action. Mr Fisher, who had inserted the mesh, suggested she should have part of her bowel removed with the insertion of a permanent colostomy. Unhappy with this option, Mary Anne chose to consult Mr Crow, a world-class specialist who was based three hundred miles away. This doctor's superlative surgical skill was counterpoised by his offensive, almost sociopathic, personality. She accepted his ambitious proposal to remove the mesh and create a temporary ileostomy while also performing a hysterectomy and colectomy.

During the five months wait for surgery Mary Anne's employment was terminated. She realised she was unable to physically and financially cope with looking after all her animals. She had to make some very difficult decisions. Her second dog, Bonny, was rehomed with a loving family, while her horse, Charlie, was adopted by a woman who Mary Anne knew would love him as she did. She found it almost unbearable to part with them; they had been with her through her darkest days.

At last Mary Anne underwent major surgery to remove the mesh. It was only a partial success due to the poor state of her pelvic cavity.

> It was so inflamed and infected that the surgery was dangerous. Mr Crow told me he'd been close to killing me from perforation or haemorrhage and that the reason I was in this mess was because the initial surgery had been undertaken incorrectly.

She explored the possibility of legal proceedings for delayed diagnosis and harm, neglect, surgical error and product liability. In spite of his words to her, Mr Crow refused to provide a statement to support her case, telling her there was no point in the legal proceedings. Instead, she should abandon these and get on with her life. This seemed like an abuse of power and a stitch-up.

In a devastating blow, Mary Anne's GP, Dr Wong, refused to see her and wrongfully accused her of pursuing freelance work while claiming her pension despite her continuing ill health. Her accusations were absurd, baseless nonsense. Mary Anne assured Dr Wong that she attached no blame to her for what had happened, but it was clear Dr Wong was concerned about becoming embroiled in a legal case. She refused to see Mary Anne again.

> *Was she so frightened she was willing to abandon her Hippocratic oath: 'the utmost respect for human life from its beginning, making the care of your patient your first concern'?*

It seemed Dr Wong's first concern was to protect herself.

> *It is not I who am strong, it is reason, it is truth.*
> **Emile Zola**

Intuitive Wisdom

> *I slowly travelled through the longest season of suffering. I battled with my inner conflicts and moral failures: rejection, abandonment and humiliation, abuse, loss and my own imperfections. But I was still grateful for the present. I surrendered to God's loving grace and mercy.*

Necessary surgical changes to your body, while life-saving, can also have a negative impact on your body image and self-esteem. This is a natural reaction to what has taken place. It will take time and self-compassion to adjust and accept these changes.

There have been several occasions throughout my life when I have learned to smile through pain in order to cope with physical and psychological suffering. I was so afraid of further harm, rejection and abandonment should I express my true feelings that I denied the pain and shame.

※

Treasured possessions may need to be sacrificed during times of hardship. You will be blessed for your willingness to detach yourself from material wealth in order to sustain yourself.

The cynical images of lazy benefit scroungers depicted by the media are a myth. This is political propaganda – harsh and vulgar.

Homelessness and poverty are not reserved for the undeserving, unlovable and marginalised. Each of us is at the mercy of these destructive events. It is not 'Why me?' but 'Why *not* me?'

※

During a life crisis there are those friends who will offer unhelpful rhetoric, which induces further pain, shame and blame. From their utopian world view they will act as your judge and jury. *All this mess is your fault.*

Your past failures dating back over many years can be used to justify others' poor opinion of you, thereby elevating their lives and egos. Harboured resentments, jealousies and disappointments are projected onto you and so add to your anguish.

The illusion of loyalty slowly fades as you realise their loveless friendship has paraded as shallow compassion over the years.

> *Times of struggle and suffering can also be the most beautiful as you are stripped of false illusions.*

※

When you are vulnerable, sick or desperate, spend time with folk who will quietly or modestly help you navigate an unforeseen river of suffering by small acts of loving-kindness. These are your true mat carriers.

Your human mat carriers selflessly provide compassionate support, non-judgemental company and love. They give of themselves and supply practical, emotional and spiritual care. It is love and kindness for love and kindness' sake. Their inner beauty and emotional generosity will help to carry you across this river of suffering.

This unusual authentic relationship can challenge and transform your perception of friendship. Where it has previously been assumed close friends would provide loving support by virtue of shared history, there is an uncomfortable realisation how untrue this can be. It's rather like a child discovering there is no such thing as Father Christmas.

Instead, folk we share no past with can prove to be a silent, gentle shelter from pain and suffering.

Nostalgic images of loyal loving soul friends, both people and pets, can soothe and comfort you at times when you are isolated, weak and vulnerable.

> *Finally, brothers and sisters, whatever is true, whatever is honourable, whatever is just, whatever is pure, whatever is pleasing, whatever is commendable, if there is any excellence and if there is anything worthy of praise, think about these things.*
> **Philippians 4:8-9**

When facing mounting disappointments, losses and fear, turn your back on them and hold on to your deepest longings and richest dreams. Trust these will lift you out of misery and carry you away from difficulty. You may soon find yourself on prosperous sacred ground.

When you feel vulnerable and devoid of any sense of wisdom, trust that you are being kept safe and held by an invisible sense of grace and mercy. Your angels are watching, waiting and ensuring all will be well.

Surround yourself with beautiful countryside of rolling fields, streams, magical woods and wildlife. Find refuge in the natural world where its peace and beauty can shield you from life's difficulties.

Let the silent clear-eyed presence of animals guide you to an inner place of soothing rest, comfort and peace.

Mindfulness teaches us that our senses truly are the threshold to the soul.

Developing Deeper Consciousness and Taking Compassionate Action

> *My body is the guardian of stories of truth – it never lies; it will tell of the disregard and indignity I had been subjected to by the medical profession.*

How does the body tell stories about our true selves?

> *During a personal life crisis often accompanied by chaos, there are those friends who will offer unhelpful rhetoric which induces further pain, shame and blame. From their utopian world view they will act as your judge and jury. All this mess is your fault.*

Can you recall a time of vulnerability when you have felt judged and criticised by someone close to you?

What effect did this have on you and your relationship with them?

Were you able to discuss this with them so they were aware of your feelings? If not, why not?

Can you recall a time when you have received love and care from a stranger?

What effect did this have on you? What were your thoughts and feelings?

Who could you describe as your mat carriers from a time when you have felt vulnerable? Are there any surprises when considering those who supported you?

How did they carry you to a place of beauty, hope, healing and peace?

Do you believe media images portraying benefit claimants as lazy scroungers is propaganda?

How can we as a society encourage one another to be less judgemental and show greater compassion to the less fortunate?

> *Surround yourself with beautiful countryside of rolling fields, streams, magical woods and wildlife. Find refuge in the natural world where its peace and beauty can shield you from life's difficulties.*

Can you recall a similar experience from your own life, in which the beauty of the natural world has provided solace?

How can you avoid being distracted and preoccupied, which can lead you to overlook the immediate beauty in your surroundings?

Mindfulness

Mindfulness is the practice of training your mind to concentrate on the present moment, while calmly acknowledging your thoughts and feelings without judgement.

> *Mindfulness teaches us that our senses truly are the threshold to the soul.*

Take a few minutes to practise this each day.

Chapter 25

The Song of the Nightingale ~ After winter must come spring

(2014 – 2017)

> *Winter within my soul was dying. I seemed to be living through the completion of several endings: marriage, career, health and friendships, both human and pets. It was a peculiar time, as I felt both relieved and bereft. The days seemed to crawl as I struggled to see beyond a dark and fallow emotional landscape.*

After the turmoil of recent months Mary Anne began to experience a time of healing and transformation. As she walked in the beauty of nature, enjoying the solitude of her new cottage, she slowly let go of harmful memories and began to find peace.

> *I befriended the unknown and yielded to its call.*

She visited a Christian retreat with a friend, where a talk from a Baptist minister came to take on great significance for her, although at first she paid little attention to his address. The man described how he had met his wife at a football match, a chance meeting that completely transformed his life. His message: 'Never underestimate what may result from a single encounter.'

Mary Anne spent many hours in quiet contemplation. As she meditated, she realised her desire to find love and to be loved was still burning bright. The thought came to her like an epiphany. Was there a last chance to find her true other, her soul mate?

After reading a magazine article about internet dating, Mary Anne decided to give it a try. She was nervous and hesitant. Initially her searches seemed futile.

> *Many of the profiles were banal and tedious, despite their portfolios of solvency and rapture. Boastful men whose age was betrayed by the story sketched on their faces described their pseudo-colourful lives as bursting with adventure.*

Mary Anne was not convinced!

But on October 3, 2014, after a morning walk around her village, she wearily opened her laptop and saw for the first time the man she had been searching for all her life.

> *There before me was a face I had not seen before but I recognised. The universe at last had conspired to bring us back together. He had a masculine beauty and radiance I knew and understood.*

Mary Anne carefully read his profile to discover it was astoundingly similar to her own: the same values, the same attitude to life, a love of nature, a love of music. He was also honest, open and self-aware. His name was James.

Mary Anne and James exchanged emails and then telephone calls that were easy, full of fun and genuine affection. They loved each other even before they met – and both knew the feeling was mutual.

> *Our first sumptuous telephone conversation lasted four hours and our first date twelve. James arrived carrying a chocolate torte, which he had made himself and decorated with a white sugar heart, along with a bunch of perfumed lilies.*

For the first time in her turbulent life Mary Anne was truly loved and cherished for who she really was. James' devotion and unconditional love would allow her to finally be her true self without fear of reproach or ridicule.

> *On 1 January 2015 James proposed to me and on 25 July 2015 we were married. It was a simple, graceful ceremony surrounded by close family and*

> *friends. There was a beauty which manifested itself throughout the entire day.*

Mary Anne and James began a new life together in a rural village surrounded by beautiful panoramic views. On a summer's walk one day, Mary Anne suddenly realised she recognised the landscape. It was the memory of a half-forgotten dream from her childhood, a dream of living in wild places with green hills, clear running water and wonderful wildlife. She knew this was where she was meant to be.

Intuitive Wisdom

> *The rubble of unfulfilled hopes and dreams surrounded me as I found myself once again kneeling at the foot of the crucified Christ. This was no icon of beauty but a mysterious place of sorrow, suffering and compassion.*

When your life seems like a barren wilderness of broken promises littered with the bitter mystery of unanswered prayers, you may also be blessed by noticing an ever-increasing awareness of life's brevity and the delicate fragility of your existence. This can enable you to grow in gratitude instead of self-pity.

This is the time to pray for the emergence of a broader hope and kinder light.

During the turbulent unfolding narrative of your life you may start to slowly realise the painful chaos associated with the interruptions and disruptions of loss are in fact a shedding of internal images of an egocentric idealised life embellished by addictive illusions.

In quiet solitude nestle yourself away from the toils of social gratification, popularity and public image. Then you will sense this is a time of healing transformation and resurrection.

> *Each morning, deep within the delicate sound of silence, wake to the beating heart of your deep longings.*

In the ordinary moments you will discover a divine presence guiding and protecting you.

Trust in your own deep-seeking, non-rational inner wisdom, also known as faith.

Wander through grassy fields, silent woods and purple-carpeted moorland. Watch floating clouds and silver streams with quiet eyes and notice how your heart sings to the beautiful call of wild birds in soft flight.

God is both 'out there' and carried within. God herself is your counsellor: 'At night my innermost being instructs me,' says the psalmist. The secret mystery of God will deepen day by day, night by night.

> *How vast and wild the night is, full of wonders, mystery and magic.*

Deep longings can begin to stir in quiet places of solitude. Their fulfilment cannot be forced. Wait patiently and listen to your profound desire to be loved.

To resist or deny your deep longing would be an act of self-neglect.

Mysterious forces and life events can conspire to prevent you from finding your one true love, your soul mate, your *anam cara*. You each carry a never fading memory of one another. Although silent at times, but always faithful and true, an invisible guide can lead you back together. Love opens the door of ancient recognition. You enter. You come home to each other at last. Each of you comes out of the loneliness of exile and home to the house of belonging.

Loving your true love is natural and effortless, like breathing fresh pure alpine air or gently floating in an endless warm sea. The effect leaves you with a deep vitality and undiscovered energy.

Life's journey can herald dramatic change. This is also known as serendipity. It can become an epiphany of luminosity as a divine spring within your soul is about to burst into life. It's as though a stream which has been long underground is searching for light and air. You will be blessed by unforeseen happiness and exciting possibilities which create new horizons wanting to be seen.

Do not squander your dreams on the manipulations of self-adulating selfish people. Instead, use your deep-seeking, non-rational inner wisdom to surround yourself with emotionally intelligent, kind, humble, tender-hearted and compassionate folk.

Befriend the unknown and yield to its call.

Fairy tales and dreams can come true, prayers can be answered and your soul will sing with grace, beauty, deeper gratitude and love.

Sometimes we look to heaven and the stars for inspiration. But ultimately the answers lie within.

James writes

As the story of the Nightingale reaches its close, it is fitting that the last words come from James. He ends his summary of Mary Anne's journey by describing a profound contrast between the last two chapters – from abject despair to fresh hope and new beginnings.

Mary Anne's story is both ordinary and extraordinary. Ordinary because she was searching for the same things many of us search for: love, understanding and purpose; and extraordinary because she had to go through hell to find them. She survived the traumas, the chaos, the abuse. She triumphed over adversity to now, finally, live life full of love, grace and peace.

The contrast between Chapter 24 and Chapter 25 is stark. It can be seen as one horrendous step backwards and two glorious steps forward.

Chapter 24 shows us that, no matter how successful and happy we might be, our fragile and precarious circumstances can so easily change. For Mary Anne her marriage, health, career, home and friendships (human and animal) were suddenly gone leaving her fighting for survival. Conversely, Chapter 25 reveals to us that life can unexpectedly switch into a more prosperous place blessed by beauty, hope and love.

In a sense, these two chapters are about life correcting itself. Mary Anne goes from the depths of despair to finding love and peace for the first time in her life. Whatever we choose to name it – fate, divine intervention, karma, faith, miracles – there is also a strong human character element, with Mary Anne showing relentless self-determination and realistic hope. She constantly chooses to make changes to improve her life despite loss and grief. She never gives up (not now, not ever) on finding a better and more fulfilling life for herself.

Meditations

As we reach the end of the Nightingale's journey, I offer you these meditations. Try to give yourself permission to distance yourself from the busyness and distractions of day-to-day living to reflect. I hope you will discover insight, wisdom, compassion and lightness of heart as you quietly focus on each meditation.

Sit down alone and in silence.

Close your eyes and lower your head.

Breathe out gently and imagine yourself looking into your own heart.

As you reflect on the following, notice how you respond and consider what each one means to you:

Deepen your awareness of life's brevity and the delicate fragility of your existence.

Abandon any traces of self-preoccupation and grow in gratitude.

Allow chaos and loss to banish yearnings for an egocentric existence defined by addictive illusions.

In quiet solitude nestle yourself away from the toils of social gratification, popularity and public image.

In the ordinary moments discover a divine presence guiding and protecting you.

Trust in your own deep-seeking, non-rational inner wisdom.

Wander through the natural world and notice how your heart sings to the beautiful call of wild birds in soft flight.

Discover how vast and wild the night is, full of wonders, mystery and magic.

Live amongst shy, authentic folk unaffected by greed and externality.

Listen to the delicate sound of silence, wake to the beating heart of your deep longings.

Befriend your profound desire to love and be loved.

Avoid acts of self-neglect which resist or deny your deep longings for love and peace.

Become aware of mysterious forces and life events which can conspire to prevent you from living a life of vitality.

Allow yourself to be blessed by unforeseen happiness and exciting possibilities which create new horizons waiting to be seen.

Do not squander your dreams on the manipulations of self-adulating selfish people.

Use your deep-seeking, non-rational inner wisdom to surround yourself with emotionally intelligent, humble, tender-hearted and compassionate folk.

Each morning, deep within the delicate sound of silence, listen to the unknown and yield to its call.

The foot of the crucified Christ is no icon of beauty but a mysterious place of sorrow, suffering and compassion.

The bitter mystery of unanswered prayers.

This is the time for a broader hope and kinder light.

Pray for a time of healing transformation and resurrection.

Discover a divine presence in the ordinariness of the sacred.

Non-rational inner wisdom also known as faith.

God is both out there and carried within.

God herself is your counsellor.

The night is full of wonders, mystery and magic.

An invisible guide can lead you.

Your life can become an epiphany of luminosity as a divine spring within your soul bursts into life.

Fairy tales and dreams can come true.

Prayers can be answered and your soul will sing with grace, beauty, deeper gratitude and love.

Sometimes we look to heaven and the stars for inspiration. But ultimately the answers lie within.

Choose a selection of these which appeal to you. Perhaps these are what you would like to become more aware of, such as the delicate sound of silence or God is both out there and carried within.

Now consider ways you can put your chosen meditations into practice. But it could just be that you give yourself permission to go out into nature more often or visit a place of worship. There is no right or wrong way, it's just the doing that matters.

You may need the support and guidance of a wise and faithful friend.

Part II

Echoes of Wisdom

A Deeper Understanding

> *I took some time out to reflect on my experience over the summer. Sitting quietly on the beach in the early autumn haze, calmly gazing across the rolling waves, breathing in the fragrant sea air, I slowly began to reconstruct what had happened throughout my stay. I began to look deeply into the rubble of my life, and I soon uncovered pieces of knowledge about myself. There was a stranger living in me, a young woman with a gentle and quiet spirit. I befriended her and listened. This was my true self calling out, showing me the way.*

Social withdrawal and contemplation can bring fresh insights, self-knowledge and enlightenment.

Use your natural instincts to gain insight into your true self. Think deeply and be creative.

During times of intense suffering the centrality of your ego is stripped of its power to delude you. You can choose to be transformed into a kinder, more loving and happier person. It will lead you to a place of equanimity and sanctity.

It is only in showing ourselves as we truly are that we may genuinely give ourselves to other people.

When faced with poor opportunities and miserable circumstances, which can be chaotic and oppressive, believe and strive for something better. Create a vision for a happier life and dream it will come true.

The path to escaping a chaotic and oppressive homelife:
- ✯ Find a safe place to live. Accommodation with food and shelter from life's storms is essential.
- ✯ Combine this with learning and supportive leadership.
- ✯ Develop a healthy routine with structure and purpose, setting priorities and boundaries.
- ✯ Seek work which involves serving others. A strong work ethic will help to develop your self-confidence, self-esteem and self-respect.
- ✯ Connect with others who value you to bring transformative healing, increased self-worth, optimism and inner contentment.

The human condition is full of contradictions. Learn to love and accept these as they gently teach you about your true self. Learn to listen and trust in your inner voice – your true authentic self. Accept nothing less.

Resist compulsiveness, harboured resentments and obsessive patterns of thinking. Trade these for openness, learning and self-development.

Remember, life is a compromise.

Choose to live by your essence and not your ego. An unlived life full of unfulfilled yearnings which is safe and comfortable with its own habits and repetitions will deprive you of freedom and creativity.

Foster self-determination and waste your heart no more on fear and vain petty preoccupations.

Be patient and empathetic with the reality of your life. Search for patterns of meaning and inner wisdom will grow.

Cultivate a spirit of enquiry; be more certain of your questions than you are of your answers and assumptions.

> *Have patience with everything unresolved in your heart and try to love the questions themselves as if*

> *they were locked rooms or books written in a very foreign language.*
>
> **Rainer Maria Rilke**
> Letters to a Young Poet

Don't be afraid of making mistakes, only repeating them. Mistakes are the foundation of truth.

Develop wise persistence, don't give in and don't give up. Be tenacious and determined.

Let go of an identity defined by past and present abuse. Transform the pain and suffering into wisdom, hope and a new way of being.

Trust that by enduring the chaos and turmoil of suffering, you will yield the fruits of wisdom, happiness and peace.

Ask only questions to help deepen the other's understanding and not to satisfy your curiosity. This will subdue the dominance of your ego.

> *Watch your thoughts, they become your words;*
> *watch your words, they become your actions;*
> *watch your actions, they become your habits;*
> *watch your habits, they become your character;*
> *watch your character, it becomes your destiny.*
>
> **Lao Tzu**

There is a weariness from unattended suffering and unshed tears. Find a healing space and skilled helpers to guide you through your pain.

Don't try to fix what is permanently broken. Instead, find time for healing and acceptance.

Your body can become tired of self-neglect. Listen to your true inner self, which may be in need of nourishing care and rest. To ignore this is a form of self-harm.

Self-esteem, health and wellbeing and ultimately inner peace and happiness will grow from self-examination, self-development, learning and education.

Avoid transmitting your own inner chaos and pain onto others. This habit can be insidious and destructive. Develop an inner awareness so as to use your suffering to transform your heart and mind and to become a kinder, happier and more loving person.

Suffering can evoke feelings of powerlessness, vulnerability, failure and abandonment. It is a time of regenerative darkness. In the silence of darkness patiently expect new life to emerge.

Avoid those who are...
- Manipulative
- Energy draining
- Self-centred
- Complainers and always moaning
- Jealous and envious
- Critical and judgemental

Forming a deep bond with someone creates intimacy and connection, but it can also blind and distort your judgement.

Be determined, hopeful and strive for all that you long for.

Find your deep hidden potential and use this to transform your dreams into the life you long for.

Strength, determination and resilience are to be found in our darkest moments: times of oppression, humiliation, failure, rejection and abandonment.

Do not be silenced by shame, which can be a harmful feeling of worthlessness.

Be comfortable with your own silence.

Good people are vulnerable to suffering. Life is filled with pain, disillusionment and absurdity. This is overcome by love, which is gentle, kind, gracious, brave and trustworthy.

Avoid becoming trapped by shame and the stigma of family mental illness.

Resist giving power and control to the brokenness of your past. Tell yourself you will not be debilitated by failure. You are not defined by history speckled by harm and abuse.

Instead, embrace the strength and resilience created by the pain and suffering of past hurts.

Avoid letting dark worries lie in hibernation like dormice curled up asleep in their nest next to hazelnuts. This could lead to a long winter for your soul encased in a silent frozen climate. Address them before it's too late.

Without strong boundaries, if you are an empathic listener showing respect and kindness you are in danger of becoming emotionally exhausted. Giving out to others who are shedding their problems onto you can lead to stress and burn-out.

Do not be a slave to the good opinion of others, especially on social media. This is a form of validation for the vanities of our small self (ego).

You cannot thrive if you live in the past with all its pain, suffering, unfulfilled hopes and dreams.

Abandon harmful memories preserved within the inner recesses of your mind. Only by discarding these can you create room for new life and prosperous beginnings.

May you wake each day with a calm mind and a hopeful heart.

Enlightenment, Compassion and Contentment

My experience in the hotel had served a purpose, showing me the way into nursing, but most of my learning lay hidden beneath the debris at home amid the dreadful human suffering and abuse. Later, throughout my nursing career, I would come to realise how caring for Mum (with her drug and alcohol addictions) taught me tolerance and compassion, while others offered only prejudice and indifference.

Be ready. Enlightenment can visit at any time and any place. Its message can be clear and life changing.

Enlightenment may not always reveal the path that you had hoped for. Instead, it may warn of future hardships which may make you feel uncomfortable. This is an opportunity to gain wisdom and courage.

Yearn to be compassionate, tolerant, humble and forgiving and resist all that denies you these gifts.

Deep suffering can evoke empathy: we can feel others' pain and suffering.

Suffering is an opening for the need and desire for love.

The need to care and humbly love another living being can help prevent the darkness of mental illness.

Learn how to love well.

Surround yourself with kind, loving people.

There is a deeper connection and comfort within as you become reconciled with those who have harmed you. Then you can begin to relate to other people with greater tolerance, deeper understanding and compassion.

Be curious about the mystery of human behaviour and emotions. This will enable you to relate to people with greater authenticity, compassion and wisdom.

Accede to ambiguity and paradox. When we come to recognise that life is imperfect we find freedom from the illusion of perfection.

Making dispassionate wise decisions, which ultimately protect all concerned, may necessitate delayed self-gratification.

It's only by discovering our truth that we can make choices for our good and the good of the world.

Trust in the invisible nature of wisdom and intuition, which guide and enable us to make beneficial decisions. There is always a choice. We have the freedom to choose and make life-changing and ultimately life-enhancing decisions.

Deep sensitivity born from suffering can enhance intimate communication. You will be more aware of subtle cues and ambivalences in others.

No matter how difficult the circumstances, compassion and empathy can always be expressed. Sooner or later we will all suffer and this can be alleviated by loving gentle kindness. Non-judgemental positive regard can help transform and heal wounds, giving hope for a happier and healthier life.

Courage is not the absence of fear.

To resist fear is a necessary act in pursuit of your destiny. Search for your inner strength; trust that you will be given all that you long for.

When you learn to master your fears, you become the master of your own life.

Recognise what you are feeling and learn to manage those feelings more successfully. Contentment is beckoning.

Try to create clear boundaries which distance you from negative relationships and toxic situations.

Choose those who validate, forgive, affirm and inspire you to become a better person.

Try to pause, be kind and smile more often. Free yourself from morbid imagination; try to let every moment bring you deep gratitude and joy. Surrender to the naked now, free from distraction and trivial preoccupation.

A deeper sense of humility can grow from sadness and suffering.

Be gentle and shrewd when others offer advice. Discernment and social civility is sometimes necessary.

Aspire to be the person you were intended to be.

Pursue your one true life as all its fullness beckons.

Fear can convince you to live in a place of familiar comfort despite this being detrimental to your health both mental and physical.

Do not deny your true authentic feelings for a sphere of illusion and self-deception. It will be at your peril.

Do not despair of finding meaning from suffering, which you may never find. Instead, trust in the mourning and healing process, which will deepen your consciousness.

The human condition is full of contradictions.

There is an inner wisdom which can help you make decisions which may disappoint others but will ensure you are protected and shielded from future tragedy.

Some of us will weep for the life our wishes never had, with tears carrying sadness and loss.

You are the most important person in your life.

Shelter from human noise in a quiet place as you dream of new beginnings. Like the miracle of birth, your hopes and dreams can come true.

※

For a fulfilling life...
✧ Adopt a lifestyle of simplicity, free from competitiveness and the trappings of modern living.
✧ Develop a sense of humility and compassion.
✧ Be concerned about social justice.
✧ Honour and revere the natural world of animals, birds, plants and trees.
✧ Watch how beauty manifests in each other, the seasons and in the natural world that surrounds you.
✧ Love and serve others with a generous, forgiving heart.
✧ Have the courage to resist that which is artificial, superficial and disingenuous.
✧ Be brave and seek your heart's desires.
✧ Make a commitment and wait patiently for the universe to conspire to make your dreams come true.

※

Like the homeless person who may shoplift to survive, desperate people do desperate things. This is a call for compassion and kindness, not retribution.
Adversity can change us for the better.

Despite your shattered dreams and forgotten hopes, trust that all will be well. Persevere. Keep believing.

Don't give up on becoming who you can be. Discover your true self in pursuit of psychological and spiritual wholeness.

If we did not love, then we would not exist.

> *Sweet are the uses of adversity,*
> *Which, like the toad, ugly and venomous,*
> *Wears yet a precious jewel in his head;*
> *And this our life, exempt from public haunt,*
> *Finds tongues in trees, books in the running brooks,*
> *Sermons in stones, and good in everything.*
>
> **William Shakespeare**
> As You Like It

The Mystery, Magic and Wonder of Beauty

It seemed to stand still in time, its long sandy beach and picturesque harbour bordered by a dramatically beautiful estuary. Immediately behind the town were spectacular mountains. There were walks and trails into places of wild beauty; ancient follies kept secret stories and scandals of mystery and intrigue.

Beauty is the divine breath that awakens the heart to new horizons.

When beauty visits, the soul is strengthened.

What purpose does beauty serve, other than to bring joy and delight?

May you sleep undisturbed with dreams of beauty and love.

Be patient with uncertainty, paradox and ambiguity. The beauty of life is filled with subtlety, contradiction and nuance.

Beauty can coexist with pain and suffering.

Suffering is not the end. Light, beauty and hope are stronger and more powerful.

Create a beautiful melody for your life. Resist all that is not life enhancing.

In the quiet rhythm of an unassuming place, surrender to a slow, hesitant beauty and grace. With no conscious effort, gently let go of harmful memories and begin to hear an ancient, inescapable echo of divine love calling you to a place of comfort, hope and healing.

Find freedom from scepticism and prejudice by searching for natural beauty, truth and love.

Learn to love ordinary days which are graced with beauty, kindness and love.

Amazing Grace – Awakening the Soul

> *I was unaware of divine grace following me until my soul felt its pressure forcing me to turn to Her in that never-ending pursuit. I gave up resisting and surrendered to God's untiring labour of love. My spirit became enlightened as I stepped into a new way of being.*

We each carry a divine plan for a life of goodness, truth and peace.

We all long to love and be loved unconditionally: free from achievement, duty, expectation, gain and exploitation. Deep within is a longing for union with the divine who manifests herself in the natural world and human life.

Our soul has a persistent yearning to be in nature; the beauty of the natural world is always beckoning.

Dreams invent your future.

During times of spiritual darkness be patient and brave. This is a time of regenerative growth and renewal.

We are sometimes guided by a prophetic whisper and a deep sense of knowing we are being taken care of in times of trouble and uncertainty.

Rest and refresh your soul in a place where time seems to deepen in an atmosphere of divine kindness and beauty.

When making crucial life decisions your faith will teach you to trust in God's wisdom, grace and mercy.

We each carry an inner guide, an inner ache, a longing to live life to the full. This ache will lead to fresh opportunities. A faint whisper is calling you.

There is sacredness in our wounds and brokenness and these can become a source of strength and healing for others. Trust in a higher power by resisting all that is not life enhancing: fear, self-criticism, negativity, despair.

Kindness shines and glows.

Your senses are the threshold to the preservation of your soul.

Through faith you will learn to embrace spiritual paradoxes of the human and the divine with humility.

Religious indoctrination can hinder rational decision-making.

Listen with your heart so that others may find a quiet inner sacred space and time to think.

Offer empathy to strangers. You could unknowingly be a mat carrier of hope, beauty and love. You could be walking on holy ground.

Sometimes only through suffering can we sense the mystery of God in our deepest self.

God is everywhere.

Some life events and experiences can feel inevitable and preordained.

In addition to physical and psychological suffering, our soul can also suffer from terminal illness.

There is a liminal space between beauty and pain. Love happens deep within this space and is called faith.

There is a language older than words. It speaks in silence of faith, truth, hope and love.

You are infused with an invisible and invincible grace that carries you to places of beauty, hope, healing, love and compassion.

Being human is a manifestation of divine beauty.

There is a silent beauty of living alone. In the depths of peaceful solitude there is a sacred space where you can find the gracious presence of God.

Our soul withers from cold, negative emotions projected onto us. Like a neglected garden deprived of sunlight, quenching rain and the loving companionship of friendly wildlife, it can become a sad, lifeless and uninviting wilderness.

The soul blossoms and thrives from the warmth and beauty of care, kindness and affirming love.

In prayerful contemplation begin to unclutter your mind from its daily restless distractions. Banish petty worries created by your own self-absorption. An inner stillness will begin to fill your mind, freeing you from anxiety and doubt. A serene white presence will embrace you, steady as the stars in a winter's night.

In quiet solitude and mysterious tranquillity a perfect peace beckons as you free yourself of daily distractions.

To progress on a spiritual journey you will need to trust in the mystery of your life and tolerate ambiguity and paradox.

Only by faith in God can you find a hopeful light through the darkness. Despite inner chaos, confusion and pain, God is at the heart of everything, closer to you than you are to yourself.

Learn to spend time dreaming of your deepest longings and notice how your life starts to flow with energy, vitality and soulfulness.

During quiet solitude there is a power being invoked, a primal force emerging within.

Befriend the unknown and yield to its call. It will guide you to true vitality and hidden longings free from the power of pain and the distracting facade of image, ambition and fear. This is your very essence beckoning.

When you recognise your true calling, it's as though a long-concealed secret message is at last being unveiled.

There is a threshold of beginning, a betwixt and between, a liminal space of grace and expectation. Trust deeply that something good is about to happen. Hope and happiness will emerge like a fresh springtime dawn.

There are sublime moments in life when all that you long for is realised.

All around us is ethereal laughter of love and joy from angels.

Your soul friend can graciously help you navigate through life's wayward storms.

We each carry a cellar of lost dreams and memories. It is possible to delicately search through these for clues and glimpses of God's saving grace, love and mercy.

There is a divine sacred presence with an invisible embrace sheltering you from hurt and despair.

Despite our confusion, bewilderment, anger and sadness, God is always present within. Even when you are unable to be present for her, she is smiling and waiting to embrace you.

Your soul will take care of you. It is a secret inner shelter.

The fulfilment of God's dream for your life is gently dawning, even though the reality may seem just the opposite.

Dive deep into your own suffering and love, and emerge with greater compassion for the world. Learn to recognise God within yourself and in others. Learn to see God in all things.

> *Walk cheerfully across the earth and touch that of God in everyone.*
> **George Fox**

The Power and Beauty of the Natural World

> *Panoramic views stretched undisturbed across wide, open fields, home to wild birds, sheep, horses, deer and cattle. Earthy country smells lifted my senses as they became the threshold to my soul. The calls of migrating geese carried my imagination to places of wild beauty.*

Go into wild places of beauty and listen to the vastness of silence. It is here you will discover your true authentic self, away from worldly distractions.

Nature with her divine beauty is calling you into her healing, loving embrace. Her adorable remedies will bring you peace and happiness.

Our hearts and minds become inspired by the natural world.

Nature takes on its own character for those who pay attention: wind, rain, light, the voices of wildlife; each contributes to its wild beauty.

Like music, the natural world can help distance you from pain, misery and hopelessness. Both have the power to change your mood and evoke a deep sense of equanimity.

Find solace in quiet places of simplicity, beauty and nature.

Allow the awe and fragility of nature to capture your imagination.

Deep within there is a rhythm which is pre-tuned to the natural world and a longing to respond to nature.

The wisdom of the natural world can impart hope and
transformation. It brings a unique kind of inner brightness, a
luminous darkness.

※

The Devotion of Animals

> *In the shelter of my horse's warm shadow I felt safe and deeply peaceful. Within these precious paradise moments, no thought, no act and no words could disturb the deep beauty of our friendship.*

We are all destined to encounter suffering in our lives. It is when we are weak, grief-stricken, sick and vulnerable that others, including our pets and animals, can help to carry us to a place of healing, love and peace.

Simple acts of human and animal kindness and soft words can carry you to places of restoration and healing.

You will find courage, strength and support from the friendship of animals.

There is a unique and special loving-kindness found only in the quiet company of animals.

Feelings of worthlessness and emptiness can be transformed into healing love by the companionship of pets.

Discover the unique beauty and majesty of horses as they stand and quietly graze.

These magnificent beasts watch us with clear, soft, intelligent eyes and charm us into a blessed state each time we pause to watch. Their alluring graceful beauty is a calling; your deep-seeking, non-rational wisdom invites you to discover their mystery and magic.

Pursue a Life of Culture

> *Those who have the power of the nightingale love poetry and music; they respond to its power to educate and inform without indoctrination. Songs are used as a way of healing our souls and hearts. Music brings motivation and life to the depressed; it heals the wounds in our lives and soothes our spirit.*

Music is an invisible language of beauty, hope and love.

Find inspiration from music, poetry and books. Many authors, artists and musicians know what it is like to suffer and how to survive, thrive and find happiness.

Art is larger than suffering and gives form to hope, connecting us to others.

> *Books are like mirrors, they reflect back to you something you may recognise about yourself, your life and the human condition.*

Books, both fiction and non-fiction, and music are powerful art forms of healing, inspiration and transformation.

Fiction can inspire the imagination as well as improve communication and creativity. Insight into different characters' thoughts and feelings can deepen human empathy.

Non-fiction, such as memoirs, autobiographies and self-help books, can deepen our insight and awareness into the human condition. This can strengthen interpersonal relationships and reduce relational stress and conflict.

Sacred texts can awaken and guide us towards a life of spiritual wisdom. This can be life changing and life enhancing.

Dying, Death and Dust

> *Dad left nothing behind other than dust and ash to scatter among the spring flowers and beauty of the earth.*

Grief can cause a prolonged spiral of despair, affecting your work, relationships, and ultimately your health. If denied or ignored you can get caught up in a cyclone of physical, psychological and emotional brokenness. You can feel lost as your exterior and interior worlds crumble.

Following the death of a loved one you will glimpse the gifts of courage, wisdom and healing which in time will be born from the harshness of loss. If you look into your eyes, there is no bleak abandonment but faint images of light and hope.

Grief and anguish can push to the surface, insisting on expression from the innermost recesses of your heart. It can feel like the sound of darkness calling out.

Sometimes only death can bring freedom from suffering and brokenness.

Death is certain and unavoidable. So waste your life no more on trivialities and vain petty preoccupations. Instead, concentrate on loving one another.

Living With Integrity

> *Like the parable of the Good Samaritan, she sensed they believed in her worthiness, her integrity and her authenticity. Her past lies and failings didn't matter. The staff did not judge her. They acknowledged she had a genuine illness, which needed healing not condemnation. There was no shame and no blame, only love.*

Be true to your authentic self. Do not deceive; avoid empty, trite remarks.

We can betray ourselves by ignoring our true feelings so as to accommodate someone else's. Do not abandon your true self. Be resolute and courageous. Be true to who you are first and foremost. This is where your strength to endure will be found. Be true all the way through, in your words and all that you are.

Be brave and challenge stigma and discrimination. Question your cultural and political worldview.

Seeking the good opinions of others by trading your true hopes and values will not ensure you are happy.

Life can present many a moral dilemma between attachment and responsibility. You have the freedom to choose.

Help to create a kinder, more egalitarian narrative of inclusivity, tolerance and diversity. One day you may be subjected to social injustice yourself.

Don't settle for mediocrity. Strive for the best.

The virtue of integrity will bless you and keep you.

The Wisdom of a Nightingale, a poem

How did you carry on? I say,
With it all?
How were you not bent double
In grief and despair?

You came upon a songbird
you said,
He sang for you that night
The sweetest of melodies.
He surely stole your heart,
And you felt blessed.

Your very own narrator
told your story in a song
Of loss and fear,
Confusion and pain
And agonising heartache
That you knew oh so well.

But he sang about Love, too.
Boy, did he know about Love!
The ways of it, the joys of it,
The very Beauty of it,
Of how you risked your life for it
And how it was there – all along.

He sang about freedom, too,
And flying high
But always knowing keenly
How to navigate Home.

His safest of nests
Woven,
With golden threads,
Like your own life's tapestry.

Such a wise Mentor!
He taught you by night,
In sweet loving notes,
And inspired you by day,
With his gentle quietude
To forgive, not forget
And, above all, to hope.

Helped you to see that Beauty and suffering
Can sit side by side,
And reminded you
That your kindness is a gift.

His was the voice of Mother Nature
Holding your hand
And healing your heart,
Like you had nursed so many
To get well . . .

And he seemed to say
That you are strong
And have a choice
You need never be alone,
Your Union with all things
Both holy and alive
Saving you.

So what are your hopes and dreams? I wonder.
Is the best still to come?
'I've been longing for a love divine,' you say,
'A tender and forgiving
Unconditional kind of love,
And I have found it.
I see God in everything."

Lesley Young

My dear friend Lesley in response to Nightingale crafted this beautiful poem. Lesley's sweet and gentle friendship has blessed me in many ways, not least as a mat carrier during some of my darkest days.

Her loyalty and loving faithfulness are gifts that I treasure deeply. She is my soul sister.

This elegant poem beautifully captures many of the important messages from Nightingale and then blends them with the grace of this exquisite bird. It is magical and soulful. Thank you.

> *May you be blessed with charitable and benevolent enlightenment.*

The Song of the Nightingale: https://tinyurl.com/262uuxn2

Amen
Mary Anne Willow, January 2025

Acknowledgements

I wish to thank screenwriter Alan Roth for inspiring me to write again. His affirming belief in my story combined with our creative collaboration gave me the courage and passion to share these insights.

A special thank you to Helen Fazal my talented editor and friend for her faithful support throughout my writing journey. I continue to grow as a writer and be blessed by her wise guidance, literary expertise and sweet friendship.

I am especially grateful to lovely Lesley a gifted poet and loyal friend. Her unfaltering dedication to ensuring I recognise the power and importance of my storytelling has enabled me to keep writing.

A deep gratitude goes to Chris and Evleen for skilfully reading the manuscript, asking questions and offering suggestions which have enabled me to consider the content more carefully.

To Alice, Ron, Grace, Mairi and Zach who radiate God's abiding grace and love. Their friendship continues to nourish and enlighten my spiritual journey.

A special thanks to Valerie who walks alongside me as I travel the inner journey. Her wisdom and deep faith continue to teach, inspire and sustain me.

A big thank you to Judith, Jane, Sue, Lizzie and Rochelle for their beautiful loving friendship.

With a heartfelt thanks to Mark, Heidi, Rebecca, Luke and Adam my dear godson for welcoming me into their family so many years ago.

A special thank you to Kate, Olivia, Kevin and Louisa for stepping in and adopting my animals at a time of brokenness. Their abiding love of Bonny and Charlie and their faithful friendship will always be cherished.

To my precious animals for their magical friendship and unconditional love.

Finally, I wish to thank my beloved husband James for joining me in the writing of this book. Through his encouragement, inspiration and eagerness to love me I have been blessed with the life I always longed for.

The Nightingale

The nightingale has totemic significance for me. Not only am I drawn to the symbolism of this bird of love and loss but it is also the name of the founder of modern nursing, Florence Nightingale.

In 1859 Florence Nightingale wrote *Notes on Nursing*, a book that is still considered a classic. In 1860 she opened the Nightingale School for Nurses whose mission was to train nurses to work in hospitals and to care for the poor. She was an advocate for women's rights and argued strongly for the removal of restrictions that prevented women from having careers. Considering the severe constraints on the kinds of activities deemed suitable for women by Victorian society and ferocious male opposition, her achievements were truly remarkable. Without Florence Nightingale my own life path might have been very different, one which could have denied me a fulfilling and successful career.

The nightingale also carries literary symbolism; not only does its song presage love, it is also a symbol of the connection between love and death. In *Romeo and Juliet* it signifies the lovers' undying love for each other, but also that both are in mortal danger. It traditionally represents melancholy and joy, love and loss, life and death.

The nightingale will sing for its mate all through the night and thus also symbolises the spiritual person practising love and visualisation. Its sweet song brings to light what is mysterious and hidden; it gives inspiration as the harbinger of a personal dawn. It guides the listener into connecting with old beliefs and thoughts and encourages her to take charge of her mind. What is learned in the night is to be incorporated into the day. She shows us how to move through different levels of consciousness and use the inspiration of higher realms while keeping grounded. She teaches us to sing loudly – above the cacophony of the mind chatter and above what others think and say. Timid and shy at times, she can show us how to act with grace and elegance.

When it comes to parental love, the nightingale's timidity changes to a brave ferocity. She demonstrates the balance between the two, asking us whether we are sharing what we know and acting what we believe.

Those who have the power of the nightingale love poetry and music; they respond to its power to educate and inform without indoctrination. Songs are used as a way of healing our souls and hearts. Music brings motivation and life to the depressed; it heals the wounds in our lives and soothes our spirit.

The Music of the Nightingale

My first knowing encounter with music was listening to the radio as a young girl. I immediately noticed how rhythms, melodies and lyrics vibrantly evoked fresh exciting feelings and a life-giving energy. At the age of nine in 1971 one of the earliest songs I can recall was 'Maggie May' by Rod Stewart. I vividly remember watching Rod on Top of the Pops and started to feel alive in ways I had not experienced before. As Rod clutched his microphone and passionately sang this classic rock song, I was free to dance barefoot and alone around the living room, for a short while unshackled from menacing worry and fear. The genie was out of its bottle and never going back.

Often, locked away in my bedroom, this invisible gift carried my inner world away from a life of despair and abuse to a place which intrigued and captured my young heart. As I grew into my teenage years, I swapped my childhood pink blanket for a transistor radio. I eagerly listened to the infamous pirate radio, Radio Caroline as it broadcast from various ships situated around the UK and northern Europe. Legendary DJs John Peel and Annie Nightingale became my trailblazing icons. I began to realise there were exciting opportunities beckoning me away from my dystopian circumstances. It was a powerful life force. Music would unquestionably become an essential companion, my soul mate, a source of invisible beauty and inspiration.

Artists such as David Bowie, T. Rex and Stevie Wonder were some of my early favourites. From about the age of 14, I discovered a kaleidoscope of musical talent: Led Zeppelin, Pink Floyd, Neil Young, Rickie Lee Jones, Talking Heads, Debbie Harry, Patti Smith, Bruce Springsteen, Roxy Music, The Smiths, U2, The Clash and The Cure. Disillusioned by state education, these musicians inspired me to explore life beyond the school walls.

Throughout my life many eclectic musicians have continued to have a huge influence on me during some of my darkest times, but also in my most joyful moments, such as when I met and married James. The sustaining power of music is sublime.

In the words of the great music icon David Bowie...

> *Music has given me over 40 years of extraordinary experiences. I can't say that life's pains or more tragic episodes have been diminished because of it. But it's allowed me so many moments of companionship when I've been lonely and a sublime means of communication when I wanted to touch people. It's been both my doorway of perception and the house that I live in.*
>
> **David Bowie**
> Commencement Address to Berklee College of Music, 1999

More recently, in 2014, I discovered The War on Drugs, a band from Philadelphia whose award-winning music helped to save me during a time of brokenness and ill health. Their intricately detailed and immaculately produced songs undoubtedly influenced the rhythm and lyrical style of writing both *The Grace of a Nightingale* and *The Wisdom of a Nightingale*. I remain grateful and blessed by their commitment and talent – thank you.

I have compiled a playlist of my favourite artists which I would like to share with you. Certain tracks pertain to a particular time in my life, others have been chosen for their lyrics regardless of the circumstances, while some artists and bands never cease to evoke a deep sense of soulful equanimity.

> *May the powerful life force of music bless you with invisible beauty, inspiration and deep joy.*

Soundtrack to The Grace of a Nightingale:
https://tinyurl.com/3jjkaxb4

Cover Design

The covers of *The Grace of a Nightingale* and *The Wisdom of a Nightingale* tell a story involving iconography taken from nature, nursing, freedom, spirituality, animals and ancient songs. The main image of the nightingale was chosen for its association with spirituality, love, music, beauty, nature, poetry and folk stories which have been told across many cultures over the centuries. These are significant recurring themes which feature throughout my storytelling.

When I began writing my memoir I collaborated with the design team Monomo & Co in creating the concept for the cover. Our imagination was captured by the many themes that linked to the nightingale. These emerging symbols became characters which were telling their own story as they naturally evoked a deeper meaning when designing the cover illustration.

The nightingale first comes into my story when as a four-year-old child I was a patient on a Nightingale ward following throat surgery. A few years later, perhaps prophetically, I sketched Florence Nightingale, the founder of modern nursing, on my bedroom wall.

The ribbon which depicts the nightingale's song carries various important symbols derived from many of the stories in my memoir. There are three crosses: the Christian crucifix, the Franciscan Tau cross, and the emblem of the medical profession, the caduceus. There is also a horseshoe, a paw print and musical notes concealed within the ribbon, inviting the reader to search for deeper meaning in the ordinary as they read my story.

The leaves on the branch of the tree symbolise the regenerative gift of Mother Nature as she constantly renews herself. The thorns depict the pain and suffering of life and also refer to the crown of thorns worn by Jesus in a futile attempt to humiliate him. This resonates with my story as I repeatedly show how I was able to overcome adversity and humiliation by developing a determined resilience.

The typography is delicate yet strong, almost fragile but sturdy and innately feminine. These attributes mirror my character as told in my memoir.

The colour blue for *The Grace of a Nightingale* and dusky pink for *The Wisdom of a Nightingale*, then brown and white for both, are the colours of water, sky, earth and light. Dusky pink was chosen for its gentle and demure femininity. At dusk we are aware that night time is returning, as will the migrant nightingale from a secret faraway homeland. It is at night we are blessed by the sacred song of this enchanting bird. So too it is at night we search for deeper meaning to our lives, as does *The Wisdom of a Nightingale*.

At night, without request, our hopes, fears, regrets and desires visit us. Like the hidden nightingale in some deep dark woodland singing for its mate, we do not know what lurks in the dark recesses of our mind. As a nurse, it was when secluded by a womblike night-time darkness that I was struck by the depth of conversation with patients, as they gingerly disclosed deep and intimate secrets.

The linocut style illustration was chosen to give a naturalistic feel, a reminder of the beauty of the natural world we coexist in.

These beautiful, graceful, elegant covers are full of life, a reflection of the essence of my story.

Background Information

The following notes give background information on some of the key issues covered in the book. Of course they can in no way be comprehensive but are intended to give a little context to the topics that arise in Mary Anne's life story. The references to support these notes are listed in the bibliography.

Child Neglect and Abuse
The Wisdom of a Nightingale is foremost a plea for children to be respected. By looking back into our early childhood memories we can understand ourselves more deeply and grow in self-awareness. We can unravel why we react and feel the way we do today. The first three chapters of the book are intended to act as an advocate for improved holistic child protection and better children's health and wellbeing.

In December 2023 the NSPCC reported that recorded offences of adults neglecting, mistreating or assaulting children had doubled over the past five years. Half a million children suffer abuse in the UK each year.

Bullying in the Workplace
In Chapter 10 Mary Anne describes her bullying boss who turns a dream job into a nightmare. Abuse or misuse of power for purposes such as undermining, humiliating, demeaning or hurting the victim is not an easy thing to tackle. It leads to poor mental health and poor performance by the victim, jeopardising their ability to work competently and confidently.

In 2024 the Chartered Institute of Personnel and Development reported that 15% of employees in the UK experienced bullying of some kind, with 8% reporting harassment and 4% sexual harassment. The findings show how bullying can occur across a wide spectrum of behaviours, ranging from extreme forms of intimidation, such as physical violence, to more subtle forms such as an inappropriate joke or ignoring someone.

The Mental Health of Veterans

In Chapter 11, Mary Anne's brother returns from the Gulf War suffering from Post Traumatic Stress Disorder (PTSD). He is depressed and has suicidal thoughts.

PTSD due to exposure to war can be life threatening. Professional help from a trauma therapist is essential. According to Cohen Veterans Bioscience (CVB) veterans have a 57% higher risk of suicide than those who haven't served. Studies suggest that 1 in 1000 of serving British Armed Forces personnel have suffered from PTSD.

Stalking

In Chapters 12 and 13 Mary Anne describes the stalking behaviour of her first husband Andrew.

Surveys show over 90% of victims have mental health problems following their experience of being stalked. Although these harmful symptoms can deter the victim from seeking help, it is important to seek professional advice and support.

The Office for National Statistics estimates that 2.5 million people every year experience stalking in England and Wales, but data gathered by The Suzy Lamplugh trust shows that only 1.7% of cases result in a conviction.

Male Suicide

In Chapter 15 Mary Anne's father dies by taking his own life. It has recently been reported that across Canada, the US and the UK roughly 75% of deaths by suicide are men.

Nearly 12 men lose their lives to suicide every day, or approximately 4,200 suicides each year. The suicide rate for males in England and Wales increased to 17.4 deaths per 100,000 in 2023, from 16.4 deaths per 100,000 in 2022; this is the highest rate for males since 1999.

The Unemployed and the Homeless

In Chapter 16 we read about Mary Anne's experience of unemployment after seventeen years of working in the public sector. She describes how those who are unemployed can be made to feel like ragged scavengers desperate for scraps from the state banquet table.

She notices how homeless alcohol-dependent folk are often ignored by society, left to rot in their own toxic stupor. On the streets disgusted passers-by ignore them withholding even a morsel of compassion and kindness.

On a single night in autumn 2023 the annual rough sleeping snapshot estimated that nearly 4,000 people were counted as sleeping rough across England, a 25% increase on the previous year and double the number on the streets in 2010.

A study of rough sleeping in London shows 80% of those surveyed experience problems with mental health, drugs and alcohol.

Public Versus Private Healthcare
Mary Anne's period of unemployment ends when she takes a job as clinical lead in a private hospital. In Chapter 17 she exposes the different values she experiences in a system dominated by financial profit.

Private healthcare is known for offering a more timely and hospitable service to patients which can help create an impression of receiving higher standards of care. However, Mary Anne found power systems of coercion, punishment, money and status with a capacity for self-serving illusions. Veiled greed was presented as flattery to manipulate its customers' egos.

Endometriosis
At the age of 39 Mary Anne was diagnosed with severe endometriosis, a shattering blow that meant her chance of conceiving and carrying a baby to full term was now vanishingly small. Endometriosis is an aggressive benign neoplastic disease, not cancerous but nevertheless invasive. It deposits and implants endometrial tissue around various parts of the body, and these lesions are at risk of malignant transformation. In Chapter 18 she shares her pain and desolation at this diagnosis, a pain made worse by the stigma attached to her illness.

According to the charity Endometriosis UK, one in ten women of reproductive age suffer from endometriosis. On average it takes nearly nine years to get a diagnosis and the condition costs the UK economy over £8 billion a year in loss of work and healthcare costs.

Endometriosis can cause significant negative effects on an individual's mental health. Multiple studies have shown high prevalence rates of depression and anxiety for women with endometriosis. Though overlooked in published literature, stigma may be an underlying social phenomenon that catalyses diminished psychosocial wellbeing among individuals living with endometriosis. Stigma has the potential to exacerbate the negative psychological effects of endometriosis (relationships, work, sexuality) and lead to poor psychosocial wellbeing. These negative effects can start as early as adolescence.

Divorce and the Anglican Church

Since 2002 the Church has accepted that a divorced person may remarry in church 'in exceptional circumstances'. This is at the discretion of the parish priest of the church where the wedding would take place. At the time of her wedding to David, as a divorced woman Mary Anne felt stigmatised that she would be denied a church wedding through no fault of her own. However, since Andrew had since died (after their divorce), she was free to marry in church as a widow. Mary Anne headed the chapter about her wedding 'The Widowed Spinster' in protest against the Church's position and this religious dichotomy.

Miscarriage

Perhaps the most painful episode in Mary Anne's life was the ending of her longed-for pregnancy in miscarriage which she writes about in Chapter 20 'Sophia' and Chapter 21 'An Invisible Loss'. Although the pregnancy lasted only a few weeks, Mary Anne's grief was profound. She was shocked to see how miscarriage is often trivialised and shrouded in silence and shame.

According to the NHS website, it is thought that around 1 in 8 known pregnancies will end in miscarriage and most of these are in the first 12 weeks. The high incidence rate of early miscarriage can lead to health providers underestimating the effect on the mental health of both the mother and the father. Even the hospital chaplain Mary Anne called on for spiritual comfort was too busy to come to see her.

After the ending of her pregnancy, Mary Anne experienced a long and painful time of intense grief.

Culturally Toxic Organisations

In Chapter 22 Mary Anne describes how the job she loved was ruined by poor leadership. The organisation had become culturally toxic. Behind the rhetoric of the benefits of constant organisational change was the desire to wield power and control, generated through the dynamics of confusion and uncertainty. Existing structures were deliberately dismantled as staff roles and responsibilities were constantly reorganised. The sequential dynamics of these detrimental changes created intolerable chaos and confusion for staff, which made them vulnerable and eager to accept their managers' agendas. This was management by fear.

The espoused values of an organisation, such as respect, honesty and collaboration, can conflict with typical behaviours and instead cronyism, nepotism and sycophantism prevail. This can lead to inept decision-making, waste and inefficiency with a negative effect on staff morale and performance.

When commercial profit becomes the only guiding principle for staff behaviours blended with insufficient management accountability for its virtuous capability and outcomes, this neglect can lead to the demise of its ethical integrity and ultimately its success.

When an employee's psychological contract has been breached there is a mismatch between agreed and expected roles. Violations of trust and integrity create inferior performance, demotivation, lower commitment, absenteeism and greater turnover. The creeping imposition of autocratic power can erode any sense of democracy. There is a pessimistic assumption that staff are to be mistrusted as they are fundamentally lazy.

A perceived breach of a psychological contract can alter an employee's performance and commitment to an organisation as well as lead the employee to consider leaving or to actually leave an organisation.

Surgical Mesh

In Chapter 23 Mary Anne describes how she underwent experimental surgery involving the insertion of surgical mesh. The year was 2011, before surgical mesh of this type became an international medical scandal with thousands of complainants and compensation claims. Around the world there are numerous government level enquiries about the efficacy of this product. The question being asked is: was mesh brought to market prematurely without adequate clinical testing?

Although she had reservations about the surgery she was to undergo, Mary Anne trusted that by giving her informed consent she would have been given all of the information about what the treatment involved, including the benefits and risks, whether there were reasonable alternative treatments, and what would happen if treatment did not go ahead. Anything less than this would have been a criminal offence.

The campaign group Sling The Mesh has over 10,500 members and was formed to raise awareness of the risks associated with vaginal and rectal mesh surgery. On their website they state:

Mesh was rushed to market using the flimsiest of evidence. It was used for almost a decade without a specific hospital implanting code so the data held by NHS vastly underestimates the thousands of women affected. Some women are unable to walk, to work again, or to have sex, and are in significant pain every day.

In a world of medical interventions, some procedures end up having worse complications than the problem they originally set out to fix. This is the tragic case of surgical mesh, where a quick-fix medical device has become a source of profound distress for thousands experiencing the often-invisible nightmare of mesh complications.

Data suggests that more than 127,000 mesh implants were undertaken between 2008 and 2017 to treat incontinence and pelvic prolapse. A more recent study suggests there were 220,544 women eligible for inclusion.

Medical Negligence
In Chapter 24, Mary Anne's life was going through a very dark period. Her concerns about the mesh were being ignored by the medical profession. As Henry Marsh wrote in his book Do No Harm, surgeons find it difficult to admit to making mistakes, to themselves as well as to others. There are all manner of ways in which they disguise their errors and try to put the blame elsewhere. Mary Anne came very close to death and in spite of being told that the initial surgery was the cause, she found it impossible to bring a case against the doctor who inserted the mesh, as the medical profession closed ranks against her.

The doctor–patient relationship is a sacred gift protected by the Hippocratic oath: '[Have]the utmost respect for human life from its beginning, making the care of your patient your first concern.' Any violation against this is a crime against humanity.

Why does the NHS repeatedly fail to listen and respond to the first signals of harm? In the United States, the FDA issued a public health notification about the serious complications of transvaginal surgical mesh sixteen years ago.

Eventually, in August 2024, 140 women who experienced distressing side effects after getting vaginal mesh implants won payouts expected to stretch into millions of pounds in England. However, there remain tens of thousands more women who have received unnecessary, harmful interventions.

List of Helpful Organisations

Mental Health
  NHS Therapy and Counselling Service
  https://www.nhs.uk/nhs-services/mental-health-services/

Counselling and Psychotherapy
  BACP – British Association for Counselling and Psychotherapy
  https://www.bacp.co.uk/

  Mind
  https://www.mind.org.uk/

  Support After Suicide
  https://supportaftersuicide.org.uk/

  Samaritans
  https://www.samaritans.org/

Trauma
  SupportLine
  https://www.supportline.org.uk/problems/trauma/

  PTSD Post Traumatic Stress Disorder
  https://www.ptsduk.org/

Drug and Alcohol Addiction
  Alcoholics Anonymous
  https://www.alcoholics-anonymous.org.uk/

  NHS Support for Addiction
  https://www.nhs.uk/live-well/addiction-support/drug-addiction-getting-help/

NHS Alcohol Support
https://www.nhs.uk/live-well/alcohol-advice/alcohol-support/

Frank, a directory providing free practical drug advice for adults and children.
https://www.gov.uk/government/publications/frank
https://www.talktofrank.com/get-help/find-support-near-you

Nacoa
The National Association for Children of Alcoholics
https://nacoa.org.uk/

Sexual Addiction
   The Association for the Treatment of Sexual Addiction and Compulsivity
   https://atsac.org.uk/

Family Relationships
   Care for the Family
   https://www.careforthefamily.org.uk/

   Relate
   https://www.relate.org.uk/

Domestic Abuse
   National Abuse Helpline
   https://www.nationaldahelpline.org.uk/

   Victim Support
   https://www.victimsupport.org.uk/crime-info/types-crime/domestic-abuse/

Childhood Abuse
   The National Association for People Abused in Childhood
   https://napac.org.uk/

   The National Society for the Prevention of Cruelty to Children
   https://www.nspcc.org.uk/

Gender and Sexuality
  Switchboard LGTB
  https://switchboard.lgbt/

  Pride UK
  https://ukpon.lgbt/

Stalking
  Report a Stalker
  https://www.gov.uk/report-stalker

  Action Against Stalking
  https://www.actionagainststalking.org/help-and-support

  Help After Rape and Sexual Assault
  NHS
  https://www.nhs.uk/live-well/sexual-health/help-after-rape-and-sexual-assault/

  HM Government List of Helpline Services
  https://sexualabusesupport.campaign.gov.uk/

  Survivors UK
  https://www.survivorsuk.org/

  The Survivors Trust
  https://thesurvivorstrust.org/

  Stop It Now – Confidential Help and Support Helpline
  https://www.stopitnow.org.uk/have-you-been-abused/

  The Crown Prosecution Service – What Support is Available
  https://www.cps.gov.uk/rasso-guide/what-support-available-help-you-0

Grooming
  Victim Support
  https://www.victimsupport.org.uk/crime-info/types-crime/domestic-abuse/

Endometriosis UK
   Endometriosis UK
   https://www.endometriosis-uk.org/

   Miscarriage Association UK
   https://www.miscarriageassociation.org.uk/

Surgical Mesh Implants
   Sling The Mesh
   https://slingthemesh.co.uk/
   https://slingthemesh.co.uk/unveiling-the-impact-of-sling-the-mesh-on-its-9th-anniversary/

   NICE National Institute for Health and Care Excellence
   https://www.nice.org.uk/

Medical Negligence
   The Patients Association
   https://www.patients-association.org.uk/

Breast Cancer
   Cancer Research UK
   https://www.cancerresearchuk.org/

   Breast Cancer Now
   https://breastcancernow.org/

   NHS help and support for breast cancer in women
   https://www.nhs.uk/conditions/breast-cancer-in-women/help-and-support-for-breast-cancer-in-women/

   Macmillan Cancer Support
   https://www.macmillan.org.uk/

Bereavement
   UK Government Bereavement Help and Support
   https://www.gov.uk/after-a-death/bereavement-help-and-support

   Cruse Bereavement Support
   https://www.cruse.org.uk/

NHS Information – Grief after bereavement and loss
https://www.nhs.uk/mental-health/feelings-symptoms-behaviours/feelings-and-symptoms/grief-bereavement-loss/

Child Bereavement UK
https://www.childbereavementuk.org/

Bullying
The National Bullying Helpline
https://www.nationalbullyinghelpline.co.uk/

Unemployment
UK Government Help and Support
https://www.gov.uk/browse/benefits/looking-for-work

SupportLine
https://www.supportline.org.uk/problems/unemployment/

The Salvation Army
https://www.salvationarmy.org.uk/employment-plus/local-support-jobseekers

Advice Now
https://www.advicenow.org.uk/tags/unemployment

Jobcentre Plus
https://find-your-nearest-jobcentre.dwp.gov.uk/search.php

National Careers Service
https://nationalcareers.service.gov.uk/

Bibliography

Spirituality & Wisdom

Aurelius, Marcus, *The Spiritual Teachings of Marcus Aurelius* (Hodder Paperbacks, 2000)

Bach, Richard, *Jonathan Livingston Seagull: A Story* (Harper Collins Publishers, 1994)

Beattie, Tina, *Rediscovering Mary: Insights from The Gospels* (Triumph Books, 1995)

Chopra, Deepak, *How To Know God* (Rider, 2001)

Delio, Ilia, 2005, *The Humility of God: A Franciscan Perspective* (St. Anthony Messenger Press, 2005)

DeMello, Anthony, *One Minute Wisdom* (Bantam Doubleday Dell, 1985)

Holloway, Richard, *Dancing on the Edge: Making Sense of Faith in a Post-Christian Age* (Fount, 1997)

Finley, James, *Merton's Palace of Nowhere* (Ave Maria Press, 2003)

Gibran, Kahlil, *The Prophet* (Pan Books, 1991)

Hughes, Gerard W., *God of Surprises* (Darton, Longman & Todd Ltd, 1985)

Hughes, Gerard W., *God, Where Are You?* (Darton, Longman & Todd Ltd, 2010)

Israel, Martin, *Doubt: The Way of Growth* (Continuum Publishing, 1997)

Israel, Martin, *Living Alone: The Inward Journey to Fellowship* (SPCK, 1982)

Lewis, C. S., *Mere Christianity* (William Collins, 2012)

Lewis, C. S., *The Problem of Pain* (William Collins, 2012)

May, Gerald G., *The Wisdom of Wilderness* (Harper Collins Publishers, 2007)

New International Version: *The Bible* (Hodder and Stoughton, 2011)

Niemier, Roch, *In The Footsteps of Francis and Clare* (St. Anthony Messenger Press, 2006)

Nouwen, Henri, J. M., *The Inner Voice of Love* (Darton, Longman and Todd, 2014)

Nouwen, Henri, J. M., *The Wounded Healer* (Darton, Longman and Todd, 2014)

O'Donohue, John, *Anam Cara: Spiritual Wisdom from the Celtic World* (Penguin, 2023)

O'Donohue, John, *Benedictus: A Book of Blessings* (Bantam Press, 2007)

O'Donohue, John, *Eternal Echoes: Exploring Our Hunger To Belong* (Bantam Press, 1998)

O'Leary, Daniel J., *Already Within: Divining the Hidden Spring* (Columba Press, 2000)

O'Leary, Daniel J., *Prism of Love: God's Colours in Everyday Life* (Columba Press, 2016)

O'Leary, Daniel J., *Treasured and Transformed: Vision for the Heart, Understanding for the Mind* (Columba Press, 2014)

O'Leary, Daniel J., *Dancing to My Death: With the Love Called Cancer* (Columba Books, 2019)

Radcliffe, Timothy, *What is the Point of Being a Christian?* (Burns & Oates, 2005)

Rilke, Rainer Maria, *Letters to a Young Poet* (Penguin Classics, 2011)

Rohr, Richard, *Eager to Love: The Alternative Way of Francis of Assisi* (Hodder & Stoughton, 2015)

Rohr, Richard, *Immortal Diamond: The Search For Our True Self* (Society for Promoting Christian Knowledge, 2013)

Rohr, Richard, *Radical Grace: Daily Meditations*, https://cac.org/daily-meditations/

Rohr, Richard, *Things Hidden: Scripture as Spirituality* (St. Anthony Messenger Press, 2007)

Rolheiser, Ronald, *The Shattered Lantern: Rediscovering A Felt Presence of God* (Crossroad Publishing Company, 2004)

Rolheiser, Ronald, 'Misconceptions About Suicide' (27 July 2003 & 28 July 2013) www.ronrolheiser.com

Plotkin, Bill & Berry, Thomas, *Soulcraft: Crossing into the Mysteries of Nature and Psyche* (New World Library, 2003)

Stalls, Jonathon, 'What Really Frightens Us' in Evolutionary Thinking, Oneing, Vol.4, No. 2

Sister Frances Teresa, *Living the Incarnation: Praying With Francis and Clare of Assisi* (Franciscan Press, *1993*)

The Northumbria Community, *Celtic Daily Prayer: Book Two: Farther Up and Farther In* (William Collins, *2015*)

Tolle, Eckhart, *The Power of Now: A Guide to Spiritual Enlightenment*

(New World Library, 2010)
Ward, Hannah & Wild, Jennifer, *The Monastic Way: Ancient Wisdom for Contemporary Living: A book of daily readings* (Canterbury Press, 2006)
Zuercher, Suzanne, *Enneagram Spirituality: From Compulsion to Contemplation* (Ave Maria Press, 1992)

Current Affairs
Bregman, Rutger, *Utopia for Realists: And How We Can get There* (Bloomsbury Publishing, 2017)
Marsh, Henry, *Do No Harm: Stories of Life, Death and Brain Surgery* (Weidenfeld & Nicolson, 2014)
Monbiot, George, *How Did We Get Into This Mess?: Politics, Equality, Nature* (Verso, 2016)

Literature
Oliver, Mary, *New and Selected Poems: Volume One* (Beacon Press, 2004)
Shakespeare, William, *The Complete Works of William Shakespeare* (Wilco Publishing House, 2011)

Personal Development
Aron, Elaine, *The Highly Sensitive Person* (Thorsons, 2017)
Berne, Eric, *Games People Play: The Psychology of Human Relations* (Penguin Life, 2010)
Cain, Susan, *Quiet: The Power of Introverts in a World That Can't Stop Talking* (Penguin, 2013)
Egan, Gerard, Reese, Robert, J., *The Skilled Helper* (Cengage, 2019)
Kubler-Ross, Elizabeth, *On Death and Dying: What the Dying Have to Teach Doctors, Nurses, Clergy and Their Own Families* (Routledge, 2008)
Maitland, Sara, *A Book of Silence* (Granta Books, 2009)
Miller, Alice, *Breaking Down the Wall of Silence: The Liberating Experience of Facing Painful Truth* (Basic Books, 2008)
Miller, Alice, *The Body Never Lies: The Lingering Effects of Hurtful Parenting* (W.W. Norton & Company, 2006)
Miller, Alice, *The Drama of the Gifted Child: The Search for the True Self* (Virago, 2008)
Miller, Alice, *Thou Shalt Not Be Aware: Society's Betrayal of the Child* (Farrar, Straus & Giroux, 1998)
Nelson Jones, Richard, *Theory and Practice of Counselling and*

Psychotherapy, 6th Edition (Sage Publications Ltd, 2014)
Pinkola Estes, Clarissa, *Women Who Run With The Wolves: Contacting The Power of The Wild Woman* (Rider, 2008)
Rogers, Carl, *On Becoming a Person* (Robinson, 1977)
Scott Peck, M, *The Road Less Travelled* (Arrow, 1990)
Skynner, Robin, Cleese, John, *Families and How to Survive Them* (Cedar, 1993)
Van der Kolk, Bessel, *The Body Keeps The Secret* (Penguin, 2014)
Wolf, Naomi, *The Beauty Myth: How Images of Beauty Are Used Against Women* (Vintage, 1991)

Animals and Birds
Armitage, Helen, *Lady of the Loch: The Incredible Story of Britain's Oldest Osprey* (Constable & Robinson Ltd, 2011)
Gardner, Nuala, *A Friend Like Henry* (Hodder and Stoughton, 2008)
Isaacson, Rupert, *The Horse Boy: A Father's Miraculous Journey to Heal His Son* (Penguin, 2010)
Kohanov, Linda, *The Tao of Equus* (New World Library, 2001)
Lee, Sam, *The Nightingale* (Penguin Random House UK, 2021)

Leadership, Management and Ethics
Bass B.M. and Bass R., *The Bass Handbook of Leadership: Theory, Research, and Managerial Applications,* 4th Edition (The Free Press, 2008)
Bennis, W., *Why Leaders Can't Lead* (Jossey Bass, 1997)
Block, P., *Stewardship: Choosing Service Over Self-Interest* (Berrett-Koehler, 1996)
Ciulla, J. B., *Ethics: The Heart of Leadership,* 2nd Edition (Praeger, 2004)
DePree, Max, *Leading Without Power Finding Hope in the Serving Community* (Jossey Bass, 1997)
Greenleaf, Robert, K., *On Becoming a Servant Leader* (Jossey Bass, 1996)
Kouzes, J. M. Posner, B. Z., *The Leadership Challenge: How to Get Extraordinary Things Done in Organisations,* 7th Edition, (Jossey Bass, 2022)
Kouzes, J. M. and Posner, B. Z., *Credibility: How Leaders Gain and Lose It, Why People Demand It,* 2nd Edition, (Jossey Bass, 2011)
Mullins, L. Rees, G., *Management and Organisational Behaviour,* 13th Edition, (Pearson, 2023)

Northouse, P. G., *Leadership Theory and Practice,* 9th Edition, (Sage Publications Ltd, 2021)

Obholzer, A., *The Unconscious at Work: A Tavistock Approach to Making Sense of Organisational Life,* 2nd Edition, (Routledge, 2019)

Rosenbach, W. E. Taylor, *R. L.,* (Eds.) *Contemporary Issues in Leadership,* 6th Edition (Westview Press, 2005)

SanFacon, George, *A Conscious Person's Guide to the Workplace* (Trafford Publishing, 2008)

Background Information References

Child Neglect and Abuse
'106% increase in child cruelty and neglect offences in England in the past 5 years', NSPCC, 2024, https://rb.gy/tslwxe, *accessed 21 Aug. 2024*

'Statistics on child abuse', NSPCC, 2024, https://rb.gy/6ih4n5, *accessed 21 Aug. 2024*

Bullying in the Workplace
'Bullying and harassment', CIPD, 2024, https://rb.gy/p3taro, *accessed 21 Aug. 2024*

'Workplace bullying. What is it? And how do we stop it?', Psychiatry UK, 2024, https://rb.gy/oznegn, *accessed 21 Aug. 2024*

The Mental Health of Veterans
'Brain trauma and veteran suicide', Cohen Veterans Bioscience, 2023, https://rb.gy/va3wok, *accessed 21 Aug. 2024*

'PTSD in Military Personnel and Veterans in the UK', Blesma, 2023, https://shorturl.at/gIRRm, *accessed 21 Aug. 2024*

Stalking
'Fighting for my sanity', The Suzy Lamplugh Trust, 2019, https://shorturl.at/JRi2R, *accessed 21 Aug. 2024*

'Only 1.7% of stalking cases result in a conviction', The Suzy

Lamplugh Trust, 2024, https://shorturl.at/f6LEd, *accessed 21 Aug. 2024*

'Stalking: findings from the Crime Survey for England and Wales', Office for National Statistics, 2023, https://shorturl.at/adaLa, *accessed 21 Aug. 2024*

Male Suicide
https://shorturl.at/E2xr5, *accessed 21 Nov. 2024*

The Unemployed and the Homeless
'Number of people sleeping rough in England more than double when Tories came to power', Big Issue, 2024, https://tinyurl.com/4ewfmnv5, *accessed 21 Aug. 2024*

'Why is homelessness increasing?', The Connection at St Martin-in-the-Fields, 2024, https://tinyurl.com/yck38fcb, *accessed 21 Aug. 2024*

Public versus Private Healthcare
https://tinyurl.com/5n6ez3c8, *accessed 21 Aug. 2024*

Endometriosis
'Endometriosis facts and figures', 2024, Endometriosis UK, https://tinyurl.com/4s8d64ru, *accessed 21 Aug. 2024*

Missmer, Stacey A. et al, 'Impact of Endometriosis on Life-Course Potential: A Narrative Review', International Journal of General Medicine, 14:9–25 (2021), https://tinyurl.com/3vnsfd3b, *accessed 21 Aug. 2024*

'Press release: Time to end the stigma', 2024, Endometriosis UK, https://tinyurl.com/2vz62a48, *accessed 21 Aug. 2024*

Divorce and the Anglican Church
'Marriage after divorce', 2024, The Church of England, https://tinyurl.com/2sv2k9fj, *accessed 21 Aug. 2024*

Miscarriage
Cuenca, Diana, 'Pregnancy loss: Consequences for mental health', Frontiers in Global Women's Health, (2023), 4:

1266931, https://tinyurl.com/yck5jrhk, *accessed 21 Aug. 2024*

Kersting, Anette and Wagner, Birgit, 'Complicated grief after perinatal loss', Dialogues in Clinical Neuroscience, (2012), 14(2): 187–194, https://tinyurl.com/24mc5t5j, *accessed 21 Aug. 2024*

'Miscarriage', 2024, NHS.UK, https://tinyurl.com/rfeeujv5, *accessed 21 Aug. 2024*

Culturally Toxic Organisations
Healthy Minds @ Work 'The Perils of Unconscious Leadership', https://tinyurl.com/yyystfy7, *accessed 21 Aug. 2024*

The Oxford Review Briefings 'Psychological Contract: What They Are and Why They are Critical', https://tinyurl.com/4fm9dyxt, *accessed 5 Dec. 2024*

Peirce, Gretchen L. et al, 'Identifying Psychological Contract Breaches to Guide Improvements in Faculty Recruitment, Retention, and Development', American Journal of Pharmaceutical Education, (2012), 76(6): 108, https://tinyurl.com/46rzj8p8, *accessed 21 Aug. 2024*

Rasool, Samma Faiz et al, 'How Toxic Workplace Environment Affects Employee Engagement', International Journal of Environmental Research and Public Health, (2021), 18(5): 2294, https://tinyurl.com/5aeh6624, *accessed 21 Aug. 2024*

Surgical Mesh
'The Pelvic Mesh Scandal – New Redress Scheme for Patients proposed', 2024, Penningtons Manches Cooper, https://tinyurl.com/y7f86bbf, *accessed 21 Aug. 2024*

'Sling The Mesh Survey 2020', 2024, Sling The Mesh, https://tinyurl.com/4rtfsrps, *accessed 21 Aug. 2024*

Medical Negligence
Marsh, Henry, *Do No Harm: Stories of Life, Death and Brain Surgery* (Weidenfeld & Nicolson, 2014)

Index of Themes

The numbers refer to the chapters in Part l 'The Power and Wisdom of Storytelling'.

Addiction	3, 20
Alcohol abuse	3, 4, 11
Animals	21, 22
Bereavement and grief	2, 11, 15, 18, 21
Betrayal	8, 13, 20
Books	2, 3
Bullying	2, 10
Career	9, 10
Child abuse	1, 3, 4
Childlessness	21
Compassionate action	5
Counselling	12
Death	3, 9, 15, 16
Decision making	7
Divorce	12, 24
Domestic abuse	11, 14, 19, 22
Education and learning	5
Endometriosis	18
Faith	2, 4, 11, 12, 13, 14, 15, 25
Family dynamics	2, 16
Forgiveness	8, 14
Friendship	21, 24, 25
Gaslighting	19
Gender and sexuality	9
Grandparenting	2
Grooming – adult	17, 18
Grooming – child	3, 4
Horses	21, 22
Imposter syndrome	8, 10
Infidelity	5, 23

Juvenile delinquency	4
Leadership	13, 14
Marriage	10, 19
Medical negligence	23, 24
Mental illness	7, 10, 13, 14
Mesh implant scandal	20
Miscarriage	20
Natural beauty	2, 5, 7, 9, 13, 16
Nature	1, 2, 22, 25
Nursing	6
Organizational culture	19, 22
Pets	21, 22
Pornography	20
Private healthcare	17
PTSD	11, 12
Self-determination	7, 9, 17, 25
Self-discovery	5, 6
Self-image	24
Social class	9
Solitude	25
Soul friend	25
Stalking	12
Suicide	15
Teaching	4
Unemployment	16
War	8
Work ethic	5, 19

Themes by Chapter

Chapter One
Child abuse
Nature

Chapter Two
Bereavement and grief
Books
Bullying
Faith
Family dynamics
Grandparenting
Natural beauty
Nature

Chapter Three
Addiction
Alcohol abuse
Books
Child abuse
Child grooming
Death

Chapter Four
Alcohol abuse
Child abuse
Faith
Child grooming
Juvenile delinquency
Teaching

Chapter Five
Compassionate action
Education and learning
Infidelity
Natural beauty
Self-discovery
Work ethic

Chapter Six
Nursing
Self-discovery

Chapter Seven
Decision making
Mental illness
Natural beauty
Self-determination

Chapter Eight
Betrayal
Forgiveness
Imposter syndrome
War

Chapter Nine
Career
Death
Gender and sexuality
Natural beauty
Self-determination
Social class

Chapter Ten
Bullying
Career
Imposter syndrome
Marriage
Mental illness

Chapter Eleven
Alcohol abuse
Bereavement and grief
Domestic abuse
Faith
PTSD

Chapter Twelve
Counselling
Divorce
Faith
PTSD
Stalking

Chapter Thirteen
Betrayal
Faith
Leadership
Mental illness
Natural beauty

Chapter Fourteen
Domestic abuse
Faith
Forgiveness
Leadership
Mental illness

Chapter Fifteen
Bereavement and grief
Death
Faith
Suicide

Chapter Sixteen
Death
Family dynamics
Natural beauty
Unemployment

Chapter Seventeen
Adult grooming
Private healthcare
Self-determination

Chapter Eighteen
Adult grooming
Bereavement and grief
Endometriosis

Chapter Nineteen
Domestic abuse
Gaslighting
Marriage
Organisational culture
Work ethic

Chapter Twenty
Addiction
Betrayal
Mesh implant scandal
Miscarriage
Pornography

Chapter Twenty-one
Animals – pets
Bereavement and grief
Childlessness
Friendship
Horses
Natural beauty

Chapter Twenty-two
Animals – pets
Domestic abuse
Horses
Nature
Organisational culture

Chapter Twenty-three
Infidelity
Medical negligence

Chapter Twenty-four
Divorce
Friendship
Medical negligence
Self-image

Chapter Twenty-five
Faith
Friendship
Nature
Self-determination
Solitude
Soul friend

Reviews for *The Grace of a Nightingale*

"Seldom have I read a book where I have been in tears one minute, angry another, then laughing the next."

"Blisteringly beautiful"
Robin Anker-Petersen, Director of Healing for St. Andrews Episcopal Diocese

★★★★★
This book touched my soul.
"I spent several days immersing myself in this wonderfully written book. I found it to be both thought-provoking and beautifully expressed, and it touched me in a variety of significant ways."

★★★★★
Courageous.
"I read Mary Anne's book over the course of two days. I have come out the other end, having experienced Mary Anne's struggles, achievements and sheer courage, with a renewed sense of purpose, to live in the moment, love every day and be utterly thankful for my lot. Read it, and see for yourself how it will improve your outlook on life."

★★★★★
Emotive and honest.
"Thought-provoking, sad, and uplifting at the same time. I don't know how the author managed it but she dug deep within her soul to write the story. A worthy book! I'll read it again."

★★★★★
Authentic.
"A brave, yet vulnerable soul, she deserves nothing but our admiration and praise for sharing."

★★★★★
A brave, challenging and affirming book.
"I've read lots of books from many genres but not one like this. It's unique and inspirational."

★★★★★
Flawless.
"The Author's mastery of language and her flawless descriptive power are distinctive."

★★★★★
Everyone should read this book.
"Brilliant. This book makes me really appreciate my life and family, the environment I live in and my health."

Notes

Notes

Notes

Notes

Notes

Notes

Notes

Notes

Notes

Notes

Notes

Notes

Notes

Notes

Notes

www.ingramcontent.com/pod-product-compliance
Lightning Source LLC
Chambersburg PA
CBHW052136070526
44585CB00017B/1847